Augustine's Laws

REVISED & ENLARGED

NORMAN R. AUGUSTINE

REVISED & ENLARGED

Augustine's Laws

AND MAJOR SYSTEM DEVELOPMENT PROGRAMS

AMERICAN INSITUTE OF AERONAUTICS AND ASTRONAUTICS
1633 Broadway
New York, New York 10019

American Institute of Aeronautics and Astronautics, Inc.
New York, New York

Library of Congress Cataloging in Publication Data

Augustine, Norman R.
  Augustine's Laws and major system development programs.
  Revised and enlarged.
  1. Industrial project management-Anecdotes, facetiae, satire, etc.
2. Management-Anecdotes, facetiae, satire, etc. 1. Title: Laws and
major system development programs.
TL56.8.A93   1983   658.4   83-22409
ISBN 0-915928-81-7
Second Edition
Third Printing

To those many individuals,
in government and out, who through sheer ability and dedication
have achieved so very much; too often in spite of the system
intended to support them.

You can see a lot by observing.

YOGI BERRA

Preface

Insight into the problems of management is sometimes found in unexpected places. For example, A. A. Milne could well have been writing about the vicissitudes of managers of large system development activities in the opening paragraph of *Winnie-the-Pooh*: "Here is Edward Bear," he wrote, "coming downstairs now, bump, bump, bump, on the back of his head, behind Christopher Robin. It is, as far as he knows, the only way of coming downstairs, but sometimes he feels that there really is another way. . . if only he could stop bumping for a moment and think of it!"

Like bears, all too seldom do managers take the time to learn from their everyday experiences. It is much as the evidence reported by the newspaper, *Midlands of England*, regarding a problem whereby long queues of would-be passengers wishing to use the Bagnall to Greenfields bus service were being passed by drivers in half-empty busses. As reported in the above newspaper, bus company officials countered objections to this annoying practice by pointing out that "it is impossible for the drivers to keep their timetables if they must stop for passengers."

This brief treatise seeks to take a respite from the pressures of everyday schedules for a moment of introspection to see if in fact there might not be, as Edward Bear suggests, a better way. Thomas Edison even *assures* "there *is* a better way," and then counsels, "find it!"

And, indeed, there is a better way, as innumerable highly successful programs have demonstrated. Still, there remains that large set of much maligned projects which, were they ever to be documented into a movie, might best be viewed with the film run backward in order to insure a happy ending. It is largely from this latter category of programs that Augustine's Laws have been formulated. The laws are dedicated to the proposition that, with a better understanding of the history of past programs, one need only selectively repeat history in the future. In Bismarck's words, "Fools you are. . .to say you learn by your experience. . . I prefer to profit by others' mistakes and avoid the price of my own." This is in keeping with Augustine's Zeroeth Law of Aeronautics: "Never fly on an airplane with a tail number less than ten."

Perhaps the principle dilemma posed in these pages is not to managers but rather to librarians: Should the book be categorized as comedy or as tragedy? Or perhaps science friction?

Many of the tribulations which will be encountered in these pages vi

are by no means unique to defense programs but will, unfortunately, be recognized to have rather broad applicability to a variety of fields of endeavor. The author has merely elected to depart from the tradition of most Washington writers and address matters with which he has some familiarity. . . thus the concentration on the defense acquisition process.

Although treated in a sometimes tongue-in-cheek manner, the problems addressed are nonetheless unmistakably both real and deserving of attention. At times slightly irreverent toward "the system," the author hopes to improve upon that system, which has, in spite of its many pratfalls, demonstrated truly enormous inherent strength and accomplishment largely because of the dedication and native ability of those individuals who *make* it work. The author is proud to have counted those people as his associates, both in government and out, and holds an abiding respect for their courage, their integrity and their contribution.

The present volume comprises the fifth printing of these laws, with the earlier, less complete versions having originally been referred to as "The Compleat Augustine's Laws." Such is the transitory nature of immutable laws.

The author would like to express his appreciation to Paul Blumhardt and James Morrison for their assistance in collecting certain portions of the statistical data contained herein, to Pamela Seats for reviewing this manuscript and to Rhoda Glaser and Glenda McFarlin for their help in its preparation.

Table of Contents

Chapter 1

Unbounded Enthusiasm

Paper Airplanes

I read part of it all the way through.

Samuel Goldwyn

It was the twenty-fourth of December and the government had just released the Request for Proposal to industry for what many said would be a program the likes of which had never before been seen. The government always releases Requests for Proposals on the twenty-fourth of December. That is in part why "RFP" is a four-letter word. The event thus was not altogether unexpected. In fact, for over three years industry had been hard at work preparing itself for this day. Operating divisions within giant industrial firms had been forming teams with divisions from other giant industrial firms in order to compete for the impending contract. An alternative would, of course, have been to form teams with sister-divisions from their own companies; however, this is seldom done due to the difficulty of cooperating with one's competitors. But once having formed up into corporate coalitions everyone went to work putting the finishing touches on the proposal, with the engineering department struggling to grind out a market-oriented sales document, the finance department wrestling with the problem of estimating the engineering manhours that would be needed to develop a microprocessor, and the marketing department determining the program's cost which would actually be shown in the bid. It was already apparent that this would be a challenging project because of the urgent need to recover during the development effort the two-year delay which had been incurred by the government in this very important project while trying to decide whether to begin it or not. Thus came about the makings of what would prove to be, truly, a crash project.

Modern alchemists of the aerospace industry, having presumably despaired of turning lead into gold, have progressed into taking what used to be aluminum and turning it into paper. That they have done so with considerable alacrity is indicated by the fact that the most critical aerospace material is no longer cobalt, titanium or chromium, but is now widely considered to be woodpulp. This situation has not prevailed since the halcyon days of Howard Hughes' famed plywood aircraft, the Spruce Goose. In fact, the only material playing a more

3

pivotal role than paper in aerospace today is celluloid, commonly used in the thousands of viewgraphs which are required to counter would-be opponents of proposed projects by briefing them into submission.

Figure 1 relates the number of pages in typical proposals for new projects to the dollar value of the programs they potentially produce, the latter based on the program plan at the time the proposal was submitted. The points above the trend-line often correspond to programs deemed by the contractor to have significant "growth" potential (of one kind or *another*) while those below the line may have been page-limited by fiat or discounted in value by the competitors due to the likelihood of eventual program cancellation. An important underlying measure of merit for proposals which is derivable from the data shown is called the "Load Factor" (often misused to represent acceleration levels or passenger occupancy in commercial aircraft), and is found by dividing the height of the pile of paper required to compete for a project by the dollar-value of the project.

The empirically determined value of the single-copy Load Factor for programs in the multimillion-dollar range is seen to be approximately one millimeter per million. It is believed to be significant that this factor implies that the pile of paper required to compete for a billion-dollar program, assuming the traditional 50 copies are submitted, must equal the "worth" of that program as represented by a stack of "2,000-dollar" bills. The fact that there *are no* such bills should not be viewed as any particular deterrent, at least not in comparison with much of the other material that appears in proposals. Contractors are firm adherents to the views of Horace, "*Brevis esse laboro, obscurus fio,*" liberally translated, "When I struggle to be brief, I become unintelligible." The problem is that in the case of most contractors, when they *don't* struggle to be brief, they also become unintelligible.

One enthusiastic proposal manager described the end-game in the following terms: "We shipped more than 32 cases of proposals to the customer. Stacked up, the content of these cases would have made a pile at least 75-feet high. Everyone really pitched in to meet our deadline — word processors worked day and night, and 'reproduction' printed more than 284,000 pages."

The truly classic cases include the TFX, for which the total set of copies for *one bidder's* proposals submitted during the four rounds of competition reached a final height of 211 feet, and the giant cargo aircraft, the C-5A. In the latter instance, just one of the three bidders submitted a total of 1,466,346 pages weighing in at 24,927 lbs. The Request for Proposal issued by the government itself occupied 1,200 pages. . . and was later supplemented by a "*Clarification* Document"

The Grossest National Product

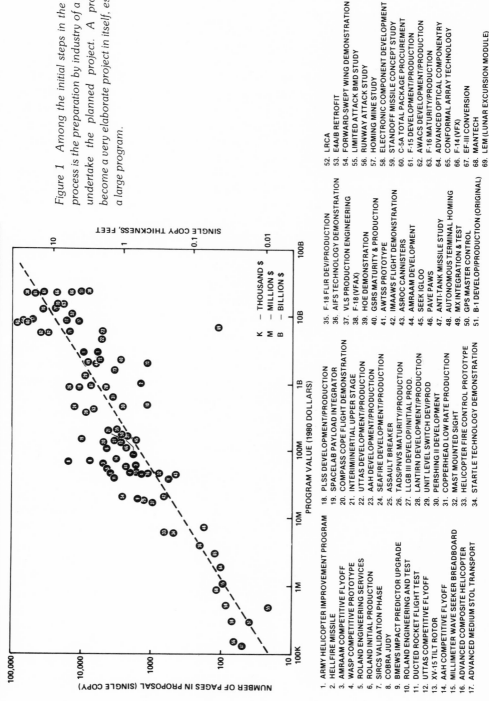

Figure 1 Among the initial steps in the contracting process is the preparation by industry of a proposal to undertake the planned project. A proposal can become a very elaborate project in itself, especially for a large program.

K — THOUSAND $
M — MILLION $
B — BILLION $

1. ARMY HELICOPTER IMPROVEMENT PROGRAM
2. HELLFIRE MISSILE
3. AMRAAM COMPETITIVE FLYOFF
4. WASP COMPETITIVE PROTOTYPE
5. ROLAND ENGINEERING SERVICES
6. ROLAND INITIAL PRODUCTION
7. SIRCS VALIDATION PHASE
8. COBRA JUDY
9. BMEWS IMPACT PREDICTOR UPGRADE
10. ROLAND ENGINEERING AND TEST
11. DUCTED ROCKET FLIGHT TEST
12. UTTAS COMPETITIVE FLYOFF
13. XV-15 TILT ROTOR
14. AAH COMPETITIVE FLYOFF
15. MILLIMETER WAVE SEEKER BREADBOARD
16. ADVANCED COMPOSITE HELICOPTER
17. ADVANCED MEDIUM STOL TRANSPORT

18. PLSS DEVELOPMENT/PRODUCTION
19. SPACELAB PAYLOAD INTEGRATOR
20. COMPASS COPE FLIGHT DEMONSTRATION
21. INTERIM/INERTIAL UPPER STAGE
22. UTTAS DEVELOPMENT/PRODUCTION
23. AAH DEVELOPMENT/PRODUCTION
24. SEAFIRE DEVELOPMENT/PRODUCTION
25. ASSAULT BREAKER
26. TADS/PNVS MATURITY/PRODUCTION
27. LLGB III DEVELOP/INITIAL PROD.
28. LANTIRN DEVELOPMENT/PRODUCTION
29. UNIT LEVEL SWITCH DEV/PROD
30. PERSHING II DEVELOPMENT
31. COPPERHEAD LOW RATE PRODUCTION
32. MAST MOUNTED SIGHT
33. HELICOPTER FIRE CONTROL PROTOTYPE
34. STARTLE TECHNOLOGY DEMONSTRATION

35. F-18 FLIR DEV/PRODUCTION
36. AIFS TECHNOLOGY DEMONSTRATION
37. VLS PRODUCTION ENGINEERING
38. F-18 (VFAX)
39. HOE DEMONSTRATION
40. GSRS MATURITY & PRODUCTION
41. AWTSS PROTOTYPE
42. IMAAWS FLIGHT DEMONSTRATION
43. ASROC CANNISTERS
44. AMRAAM DEVELOPMENT
45. SEEK IGLOO
46. PAVE PAWS
47. ANTI-TANK MISSILE STUDY
48. AUTONOMOUS TERMINAL HOMING
49. MX INTEGRATION & TEST
50. GPS MASTER CONTROL
51. B-1 DEVELOP/PRODUCTION (ORIGINAL)

52. LRCA
53. E4A/B RETROFIT
54. FORWARD-SWEPT WING DEMONSTRATION
55. LIMITED ATTACK BMD STUDY
56. RUNWAY ATTACK STUDY
57. HOMING MINE STUDY
58. ELECTRONIC COMPONENT DEVELOPMENT
59. STANDOFF MISSILE CONCEPT STUDY
60. C-5A TOTAL PACKAGE PROCUREMENT
61. F-15 DEVELOPMENT/PRODUCTION
62. AWACS DEVELOPMENT/PRODUCTION
63. F-16 MATURITY/PRODUCTION
64. ADVANCED OPTICAL COMPONENTRY
65. CONFORMAL ARRAY TECHNOLOGY
66. F-14 (VFX)
67. EF-III CONVERSION
68. MANTECH
69. LEM (LUNAR EXCURSION MODULE)

70. CX
71. S-3A
72. HARPOON
73. KC-10

of over 1,600 pages! A total of some 500 evaluators were needed to wade through the material provided by the three bidders.

"Why use one word," as the saying goes, "when ten will do?"

The degree of improvement wrought by the growing length of proposals and contracts as they have evolved over the years is suggested in the tale of two airplanes. When the Army Signal Corps purchased the development of an aircraft from the Wright Brothers, the Request for Proposal consumed fully one page; the entire contract (a fixed-price incentive type) comprised two pages. The latter was the result of a 40-day competition among 41 bidders which culminated in a 9-day evaluation period by the government. An award was made* and the aircraft flew successfully some six months later.

The primitiveness of this management system contrasts sharply with the more sophisticated approach used today which, in the case of the giant C-5A transport, generated contractor proposals the paper for which would have more than filled the C-5A itself. The recent Advanced Helicopter Improvement Program (AHIP) competition exceeded even this standard of achievement . . . with one contractor's proposals (all required copies) exceeding the takeoff weight of the helicopter. Many systems, it seems, are now quite literally worth their weight in paper. In fact, the former President of Vought Aeronautics estimated in *The Dallas Times Herald* that each time a new military airplane flew over the fence at their plant, 27 percent of its cost was attributed to paper. A single copy of a winning proposal for a modern aircraft requires a document embodying a preparation cost per pound (including the contractor-sponsored effort to develop the information) about *400* times the cost per pound of the aircraft itself.

But the above data include only the initial proposal and not all the resubmittals which often double or triple the pile which must be provided. Nor do the data include supporting documentation which must eventually be generated. . . such as the MX Environmental Impact Statement which ran a full 8,000 pages even in its draft form. One recent government publication on the marketing of cabbage contains, according to one report, 26,941 words. It is noteworthy in this regard that the Gettysburg Address contains a mere 279 words while the Lord's Prayer comprises but 67.

Fortunately, the United Nations recognized the existence of this situation and established a Committee on the Reduction of Paperwork. The Committee has now released a 219-page report concluding that paperwork should indeed be reduced. Similarly, the U.S. Commission on Federal Paperwork produced a widely distributed 74-page report, which was unfortunately soon surpassed by a 113-page

---

*Without protest.

report on the same topic generated by the succeeding administration.

Not to be outdone, the Defense Department has commendably taken steps to page-limit proposals submitted by its would-be contractors. One of the first efforts to accomplish this involved limiting proposals for one particular program to 1,000 pages. . . a laudable concept had not the government's own Request for Proposal bulged 1,114 pages. The initial response of the bidders, who for years had been complaining about the length of proposals, was not particularly commendable either; they produced documents for which the print size rivaled the best products of their microelectronics production facilities and invented "foldouts" with margins seemingly 1 Angstrom wide.

The blame for this verbosity is not, however, entirely assignable to the contractors. They, too, are often faced with a veritable flood of vagaries to which a specific and detailed response is demanded. In fact, as viewed through the eyes of competing contractors the source selection proces often appears to be somewhat an enigma wrapped in a mystery. Reluctance to state specific scoring weights to the bidders, for example, results in statements such as the following taken from one recent Request for Proposal: "The weighting of technical factors exceeds that of all other individual factors but is less in value than the sum of cost and schedule. Technical excellence is weighted more heavily than cost which in turn receives more value than schedule which is equal in value to the combination of management and past performance. No one factor represents half of the total weighted value to be used in the contractor selection."

A story in *Government Executive* magazine tells of the Undersecretary of the Army pointing out to his contract manager that the length of a recent Army Electronics Command Request for Proposal, coupled with the alotted 30-day response time, would very likely pose problems to industry. Specifically, he noted, if one were to work 24 hours a day, seven days a week, for the entire month, only ten minutes would be available to read, digest, and prepare a response to each page of the government's request!

Recent efforts to select contractors for new items of hardware conducting "flyoffs" of actual prototype hardware instead of paper engagements have produced some astonishing results. In those cases where the selection has been based upon a conventional evaluation of paper proposals, the incumbents, defined as the builder of the previous generation of the item of equipment to be replaced, won about two-thirds of the competitions. In contrast, when flyoffs of actual hardware were involved, the darkhorse (newcomer) exactly reversed the above odds, winning two times out of three.

The explanation of this happenstance has its origins in biblical times: "He multiplieth words without knowledge":Psalm 35:16. Or, in more contemporary parlance, "I should have asked the question you answered."

The overall law resulting from these considerations appropriately has its title derived from computer parlance and is known as the Law of the Core Dump:

The thickness of the proposal required to win a multimillion dollar contract is about one millimeter per million. If all the proposals conforming to this standard were piled one on top of the other at the bottom of the Grand Canyon, it would probably be a good idea.

(LAW NUMBER I)

Justice Deserts

Fool me once, shame on you.
Fool me twice, shame on me.
American Indian expression

To err is human. To forgive is against procurement policy.
Or is it? Having prepared the requisite mound of paper and
promises, the hopeful contractors pass from the stage
momentarily and the second portion of the courtship
begins. This phase belongs to the source-selection
evaluators, government employees who are assigned the
unenviable task of reviewing the mountain of material
which has been painstakingly prepared by the contenders.
The source-selection process reaches its culmination when
that decisive and divisive step having such a great sound of
finality is reached: the submission by each contractor of
what is officially known as a "Best and Final" offer but is
more aptly described by many in industry as "Last and
Worst." Unfortunately, in this project, as in many others,
the process culminated several times — as no fewer than
four successive "Best and Final" offers were solicited from
each competing contractor. The entire process had
somehow degenerated into one of "Do unto others before
they do unto you." Worse yet, it was soon to be learned
that, as George Eliott long ago noted in Silas Marner,
"Nothing is so good as it seems beforehand."

Would any private consumer continue to patronize a seller who had
just charged 50 percent more for an item than had been indicated in
the original agreement, delivered the article one-third later than
promised, and capped this off by changing the management being
dealt with three times during the course of the purchase? Not likely.
Yet this has quite literally been the norm* in the sophisticated process
of acquiring major system developments and leads to what is in-
formally referred to as the "Lemming Law of Government
Procurement." That is not to suggest that there are not many extenuating circumstances from the perspective of both the seller and

---

*The indiscreet use of this word has, on *particularly* uninspired occasions, led to these
laws being referred to as "Augustine's Norms."

9

Memory in the Source Selection Process

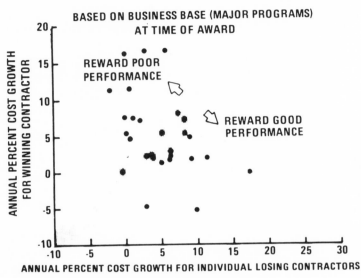

DATA SOURCE: DOD SELECTED ACQUISITION REPORTS, FIVE YEAR AVERAGE
CORRECTED FOR INFLATION & QUANTITY CHANGES

Figure 2   The process of selecting a contractor to undertake a project generally gives little formal consideration to the past records of the contending firms. Only slight correlation is found between cost control on previous contracts and the likelihood of winning future awards.

the buyer. There are. But to perpetuate a procurement policy founded, perhaps even floundered, on the virtues of amnesia would seem to be contrary to fundamentals of the Free Enterprise System.

Many contractors, explaining away disappointment with their past work, subscribe to Frank Lloyd Wright's viewpoint. "When I was 90," said Wright, "I was asked to single out my finest work. My answer was 'My *next* one.'" Similarly, if the corporate vice president of marketing points out that "we have not had a major disaster since 1955," the government project manager is unable to take much solace when a quick check of his watch reveals it is then only 2015.

Figure 2 presents evidence that whatever other problems may be attributable to the contract award process, it is at least free from discrimination. Free from discrimination, that is, in the sense that it treats good performers and poor performers with equanimity. The figure displays for a number of major source selections the relative ranking of the winning and losing bidders in terms of one important measure of past performance: the degree of cost control exhibited on their in-being major programs at the time of the subject new award. Were all the data points to cluster in the lower-right-hand corner of the figure, one might conclude that contractors which performed well in the past were more likely to win new business in the future and, likewise, that poor performers were less likely to be future winners. But, as seen from the lack of any such correlation in the data, the extant version of turning the other cheek seems merely to be to turn the other check. In essence, then, in the source-selection process the accumulation of, say, twenty years' experience more accurately corresponds to accumulating one year's experience twenty times.

These results agree with the findings of a companion qualitative investigation which rated competing contractors on all aspects of their past record (cost, schedule, performance. . .) rather than on cost alone. The correlation coefficient between winning in source selection evaluations and past performance ranking among the competitors was a mere 0.1 on a scale where zero indicates total randomness and unity indicates perfect correlation. As Carl Ajello, Attorney General of Connecticut, puts it, "History is important. If you don't know where you have been, you damn sure don't know where you are going."

The public seems to have hit upon a solution to this selection problem in the important matter of electing a President. The criterion in use is to select the taller of the two principal candidates. . . a criterion which has applied in 19 of the last 20 presidential elections.* Those who would dismiss this occurrence as a probabilistic quirk should be forewarned that on a statistical basis the odds against having so few such instances are about 50,000 to 1.

None of the above is to suggest that the assessment of past performance of politicians *or* contractors is easy . . . only that at least the latter is somehow done millions of times *every* day by housewives shopping, children buying candy and, interestingly, prime contractors dealing with *their* vendors. Real problems certainly do exist: how should a new firm with *no* track record whatsoever, *either* good or bad, be rated? How should a satisfactorily performing firm acquired by a poor performer be ranked? How should a sister division of a notoriously poor performer within the same company be treated? Or how, as actually happened in the air-launched cruise missile competition, should past performance be allocated when the president of

---

*The single departure from this rule was in 1976, when Jimmy Carter pulled a three-inch upset.

one of the competing firms suddenly becomes president of the other? Further, changes in management or even management emphasis may *more* than offset past problems; thus, the objective must always be to maximize the chances of success in the future and not merely to assure vengeance for the past. But the practice of engaging in a source selection process with *no* apparent memory of *either* past successes or transgressions would seem to perpetuate the belief that each time at bat is the beginning of a new season. . . and thereby reap all the liabilities of the widespread suspicions that the Law of the Phoenix must indeed be operative:

The source selection process is based on a system of rewards and penalties, distributed randomly.
(LAW NUMBER II)

Under such circumstances, there will inevitably be individuals who adopt a policy that "it is a pleasure to do business to you." This can, unfortunately, lead to many truly forgettable experiences.

Telling It Like It Isn't

The cause is hidden,
but the result is well known.

Ovid

The real villain in this tale begins to emerge. Its exact identity is revealed only as time passes, but its parenthood is already known to be optimism and enthusiasm and its exact heritage seems to have something to do with cost-estimating. "This is the time," according to Bert Fowler, a vice-president and General-Manager at The MITRE Corporation, "when grown men gather in a room in each company and spend their time not trying to decide what the cost would really be, but trying to guess what the grown men in the other rooms are going to guess." It's like trying to read the mind of people who haven't yet made up their mind. Each contractor evolved an intricate strategy for winning. One, a Fortune 500 industrial giant, was seeking special consideration as a "Disadvantaged Small Business Firm" — on the grounds that if it did not win it might in fact become a small business. Another was proposing a "low risk, modest upgrade" to an already existing item it had been producing (the upgrade consisting of a factor of twelve increase in weight, a factor of ten in thrust, and a factor of nine in volume. . .), a practice known as "jacking up the nameplate" in recognition of the fact that the name would indeed be preserved. Still another was encouraging the government to adopt contract terms and conditions that were so incredibly risky and onerous that all the competition would be prudent enough to drop out. But by far the most innovative strategy in this fixed-priced contest was that of the contractor which, by spreading rumors of submitting an inordinately low bid, was attempting to drive its principal competitor to reduce ITS price to a winning position. . .in the hopes that the disaster which would surely ensue would so mortally wound the hapless "winner" that it could then be purchased

13

Cost Estimation Track Record

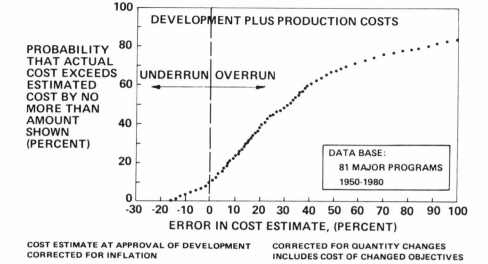

Figure 3   Estimating the cost of research and development efforts inherently involves uncertainty. This is a significant ingredient in the probabilistic character of cost growth.

lock, stock and barrel for less investment than would be required simply to win the incipient contract! All the competitors, as it happened, held the belief that it would be fortunate if the winner's honeymoon with the customer survived more than a few hours beyond the victory party. The contractor employees couldn't help but think back to the dispute which had boiled over whether to participate in so intensely competed a fixed-price development effort in the first place and how the marketing department had argued for a "no bid" decision because of a concern that the company might lose while the finance department argued for a "no bid" because of a concern that they might win. Certainly no one could argue that it had been other than a vicious competition from the very outset. There had been allegations of buy-ins and bail-outs, with the allegators in turn being accused of benefiting from leveling, leaks, and love-ins. Such practices became so flagrant that for a considerable period the possibility existed that the contract might be the very first to be awarded posthumously.

When it comes to accuracy of cost-estimating and pricing for many activities of the recent past, we were, as the saying goes, apparently expecting very little, and we certainly were not disappointed. We might even settle for mediocrity, if we could find it. In fact, the overruns in most development programs, due largely to unforeseen (as opposed to unforeseeable) tasks, were so large that, if it weren't for the bad luck embodied in those programs, they might have had no luck at all.

The habit of unjustifiably concluding, early in an undertaking, that one is in a better position than the facts warrant has been found to have spread beyond the matter of estimating cost status of new development programs. For example, a press release by an underdog Army team just before an Army-Navy game, noted: "The season began well enough, with Army taking a 10-10 lead into the fourth quarter [of its first game]." Actually, though, this proved to be quite prescient as in the Army-Navy game that ensued, the Army gained what almost all agreed was a 3-3 victory. Thus, numbers do not tell all. . . *especially* numbers pertaining to the cost status of newly initiated technological programs or other activities having a similarly high emotional content.

Law Number XXIV will later indicate how to adjust typical (i.e., wrong) cost estimates at any *perceived* point in a development program so that the correct estimate could, on the average, be determined. But what if one were not satisfied with merely being correct on the *average?* Supposing one wanted to be, say *90 percent* certain that the cost estimate for a given program would not be exceeded? What then?

Figure 3 presents historical data, corrected for inflation, concerning a large number of completed programs from which one can determine the chances of an overrun of any given magnitude occurring. It will be seen immediately that only 10 *percent* of the time were programs completed within the original cost estimate. Stated differently, contractors and their government overseers are bidding for development projects (involving presumably cost-reimbursable contracts) at about a ten-percent confidence level. How can this be? Why don't such improbable estimates stand out like fur coats on a grocery list? Particularly when programs which were terminally ill (i.e., ultimately cancelled prior to completion) have not even been included in these statistics. Viewing overruns from this perspective it should certainly be no surprise that we are frequently surprised. With this type of mathematics it can readily be seen that it would indeed be odd to come out even.

The reason, simply stated, is that the cost-estimation process as it now exists is fundamentally unstable. The forces inherent in it all act in concert to drive *estimated* costs downward to unreasonable levels. . . with seemingly no effective counterbalancing influence in existence. The contractor quite naturally wants to submit a lower cost bid than any of its competitors; the sponsoring government organization wants to obtain approval for its program from the Congress; the Congress wants to appropriate as little money as possible prior to the next election;the government's contracting department wants to demonstrate that it is a tough negotiator;and so on throughout the entire process. It is like sending lettuce by rabbit. And it is soon learned by those on both sides of the negotiating table that if you will just go 60 percent of the way, the other side will go the other 60 percent. The participants in the process may have attended different schools but they seem somehow to have attended them together. It all adds up — or, more accurately, subtracts down — to a cost estimate for the "winning" contractor which is, as has been seen, far too low. The cost *estimate* has in effect become a cost *"desirement."* In Euripides' words this would be categorized as a bad beginning making a bad ending. But in modern industrial parlance, it would be described as giving each other the business. As Sebastian Brant, who understood this problem as early as 1494, put it, "The world wants to be deceived" — and according to C. N. Bover, "The worst deluded are the self-deluded." There are sixty-two ways to underestimate costs and it has been said that bidders have not resorted to one of them. Now what needs to be done is to find out what that one is so at least some semblance of safeguard can be established.

It is thus discovered that, in mathematical terms, cost estimating deals with truly complex numbers—each having a real and an imaginary part.

The competitive bidding process pursued by the government for developmental work is such that after an initial submittal each con-tractor is given the opportunity to fix certain shortcomings identified in the review sequence. This tends to produce a "leveling" whereby the technical acceptability of all contractors becomes very close, with initial advantages having been neutralized and price thereby escalated in perceived importance. The next step is the simultaneous submittal by all contractors of a Best and Final Offer, pronounced "bafo." The real difficulty stems from those cases which, for one reason or another, generate a second, third, or even fourth "bafo." These are called, appropriately, "barfo" (best and *really* final offer) and "baarfo" (best and absolutely really final offer). But, independent of what they are called, their effect is clear; at each step along the way each contractor increases his optimism by 10 percent. An old-fashioned auction results. Although such procurement practices are avoided, some of their properties have a subtle manner of creeping into purchases.

For most programs which employ the above techniques of cost estimating, matters generally deteriorate steadily after the initial disastrous start. But this has not dissuaded a long line of managers from believing that they, unlike all their predecessors, will be able to manage their programs such that they encounter no unforeseen events—and complete the job for the specified cost. Shakespeare wrote about this kind of manager in *Henry IV, Part I* (Act III, Scene 1):

Mortimer: I can call spirits from the vasty deep.

Hotspur: Why, so can I, or so can any man; but will they come when you do call them?

One solution to this dilemma, that of incentive contracting, has on occasion been traced to the Wright Brothers' original agreement with the U.S. Army. . . which was, as has been noted, an incentive-type contract. But this solution. . . and the problem it addresses. . . were extant long before the Wright Brothers were even considering diversifying their bicycle business. It turns out, according to Marcus Vitrivious Pollio, the architect and engineer, that the ancient ancestral law in the Greek city of Ephesus demanded engineers to file a formal cost estimate with the magistrate prior to initiating work on a public project. If the work was completed for the specified amount, the engineer was rewarded with decrees and marks of honor. An overrun of up to one-fourth was financed by the treasury without the imposition of penalty. But excesses over one-fourth were drawn from the engineer's personal property which had to be pledged as security at the time of response to the RFP (Request for Proposal). As seen from Figure 3, were such a practice to be reinstated some 25 centuries later, approximately 55 percent of the engineers would be spending their nights on the steps of the Parthenon.

It is important to note that in matters entailing such enormous inherent uncertainty as research and development of sophisticated systems no one need actually be guilty of equivocation; everyone need simply be wildly optimistic. . . a disease which is highly contagious in the absence of any effective vaccine or antidote. In terms that Jimmy the Greek (if, not, sadly, many cost estimators) would most assuredly understand, to obtain a fifty-fifty chance of completing a prescribed undertaking within the estimated cost, the bid costs, determined through traditional practices of the past two decades, would have to have been increased by 31 percent. To have obtained a 90 percent confidence of not exceeding the estimate, one would have needed to increase the estimates by fully 148 percent. The disparity between these two figures, incidentally, lies at the core of the reason why fixed-price contracts are simply not suitable instruments for research and development tasks involving prescribed end-items.

Although defense acquisition projects are generally characterized by significant technological challenge on the basis of seeking to gain an edge over potential adversaries, cost-estimation problems are by no means the exclusive province of defense programs. Dulles Airport suffered an "overrun" by a factor of 1.49 when it was constructed, and the Tennessee Tombigbee Waterway by 1.76. The corresponding figure for the Appalachian Development Highway is 2.65; for the New Orleans Superdome, 3.22; and for the Trans-Alaska Pipeline, 4.25. Even the Canadian Olympics, scheduled to cost a reported $400 million, wound up costing nearly $2 billion.

Some of the all-time overrun leaders have been identified in data collected by Myron Kayton, a consulting engineer, in his studies of new-technology projects in the 19th Century. He reports the suffer-factor for the Erie Canal as 12,000 percent; for the Cincinnati-Covington bridge as 730 percent; the Hoosac Tunnel in Western Massachusetts as 2,500 percent; and the Brooklyn Bridge as a mere 85 percent. . .at least on the occasion of its *initial* sale. It would seem that to have a dismal record would require considerable improvement. No question but that misery loves company.

These data, of course, all relate only to the past and include government costs as well as contractor costs. But in spite of these limitations, there seems once again to be little reason to doubt George Santayana's admonition that "those who cannot remember the past are condemned to repeat it." And, in this respect, there would seem to be many alive and well today, particularly in the development trenches, who are suffering through at least their third reincarnation... all the while fully confident that the future will not include unhappy surprises and oblivious to the fact that the past *always* included unhappy surprises. And in this case, the past goes all the way back to the building of the Suez Canal (200 percent overrun), the Panama Canal (70 percent) and even the Roman Aquaduct (100 percent). Mercifully, the pharaohs kept only sparse records on the pyramids.

The above assessment indicates what cost estimate should be used in order to insure that, say, half the programs undertaken are completed for less than their projected cost (and the other half for more). It may be of greater significance to assure that the *money* saved on the programs which do in fact underrun is sufficient to compensate for the losses on those which suffer overruns. The above two statements are obviously not equivalent since the probability distribution is skewed. That is, a plethora of programs endure overruns of 100 percent. . .

but there is a noticeable scarcity of programs which offset this growth with *underruns* of 100 percent. It is thus seen that, as might have been expected, the odds *are* indeed odd. This is, of course, indirectly related to the principle that causes people to drown in streams having an average depth of six inches. Or, to the principle which governs the airport pick-up busses run by car rental firms; said busses arriving an *average* of every five minutes — in bunches of four.

The factor which, if applied in recent years, would have guaranteed that the house breaks even for the overall set of programs pursued can be determined approximately from the data used to prepare Figure 3. This factor equals at least 1.52 and is known as the "Las Vegas Factor of Development Program Planning." Normally it is quoted to at least seven significant figures; however, this neglects the fact that even this metric is subject to change depending upon the amount of risk that is entailed in a specific program. Graphically, this degree of hazard is represented by how flat (risky) or steep (certain) is the slope of the curve in Figure 3 for the *particular* program addressed.

One might expect, in keeping with the fundamental laws of economics—not to mention official government policies—that activities which entail the greatest risks would be those which would return the greatest profits. Quite the contrary, such highly volatile endeavors as research and development carry the smallest *realized* profit margins; routine matters such as the provision of spare parts carry the largest, and intermediate risk-bearers, such as serial production, reside, in terms of profit rate, somewhere in between.

All the above mathematical meandering can be distilled much more straightforwardly into the Law of Apocalyptic Costing:

Ninety percent of the time things will turn out worse than you expect. The other ten percent of the time you had no right to expect so much.

(LAW NUMBER III)

As the old saying goes, you have to kiss a lot of frogs to find a prince.

Those who find such statistics implausible must explain, say, why 90 percent of the world's air traffic arrives and departs from the 10 percent of the gates farthest from the terminal building.

The choice is thus straightforward: one can either face up to the true cost of an undertaking at its outset or, alternatively, parcel out the bad news on the installment plan. There simply are no other options. And in this respect, those involved in government development activities rank among the all-time great proponents of what is *said*, in some less sophisticated circles, to be referred to as the "slow reveal." "I'll think on it tomorrow. . .I can stand it then. Tomorrow I'll think of some way," said Scarlett O'Hara.

In the words of Peter Hall, in the concluding sentence of his work, *Great Planning Disasters*, "There may be some excuses for great planning disasters, but there are not nearly so many as we think."

Figure 3, of course, deals only with the matter of estimating *costs*. If one makes a similar plot showing schedule outcomes or performance (speed, range, accuracy, payload. . .) outcomes, it is found that while there is only a 10 percent chance of meeting *cost* goals, there is a 15 percent chance of meeting *schedule* goals and a 70 percent chance of satisfying *performance* goals. The long-suspected priority hierarchy is thereby mathematically derived. Performance reigns supreme. For many years it had appeared that nothing could ever make the schedule-performance record look good. That was before the cost-performance record came along.

Some 2400 years ago Thucydides got to the root of the cost-overrun problem: "Their judgment was based more on wishful thinking than on sound calculation of probabilities; for the usual thing among men is that when they want something they will, without any reflection, leave that to hope, while they will employ the full force of reason in rejecting what they find unpalatable." It is not that contractors do not *know* how to estimate costs conservatively. Nor is it that they do not know how to win competitions. The problem resides in the fact that most do not know how to do both simultaneously.

With all participants in the cost estimating process motivated more by the law of survival than the law of probability, what other outcomes could we have expected? How could we possibly be surprised? To quote astronaut Pete Conrad from Gemini XI, "We're on top of the world. You can't believe it. . . utterly fantastic. The world is round."

The fact that the government's managers *know* they have "incentivized" contractors to be optimistic in estimating costs suggests that the following conversation from Romanoff and Juliet involving a general and two ambassadors might just as well have taken place among a general and two contractors:

General: . . .Incidentally, they know your code.

American Ambassador: We know they know our code...
We only give them things we want them to know.

General: Incidentally, they know you know they know your code.

Soviet Ambassador: . . .We have known for some time that they knew we knew their code. We have acted accordingly — by pretending to be duped.

General: . . .Incidentally, you know — they know you know they know you know. . .

American Ambassador: What? Are you sure?

The problem is much as the one encountered by the businessman who discovered a card in his hotel room stating, "If you have a problem with alcoholism and need help, call 344-2920." Upon calling the number, he found that it was a liquor store.

On Making a Precise Guess

A horse that can count to ten
is a remarkable horse, not a
remarkable mathematician.
Samuel Johnson

As Benjamin Disraeli pointed out long ago, there are in-
dividuals who use statistics as a drunkard uses a lamppost:
for support rather than for illumination. This proves to be a
valuable piece of insight for the promoters of our newly
established project who must justify its very existence
armed with only the most tenuous of data. The search not
unexpectedly turns to methods of making the unknown,
indeed even the unknowable, appear plausible to those
who insist upon knowing. As luck would have it, a powerful
technique is soon discovered.

In the late 1950's a well-known Princeton geology professor answered a question which arose during a field trip about the age of a
fossil that had been found by stating it was two million and two years
old. Responding to still another question by students incredulous over
his ability to precisely date so old an object, he explained that another
group had visited the same site two years earlier and had been told by
a local farmer that the fossil was then two million years old!

As reported to the Congress at the time development was to be
initiated, the total program cost for the Harpoon program was said to
be $1,031.8 million. For the A-10 program, the corresponding cost
was defined as $2,489.7 million. Not $2,400 million; not even
$2,489 million. Rather, the cost would be two thousand four hundred
eighty-nine *point seven* million dollars.

This great degree of accuracy may perhaps be somewhat surprising
to the uninitiated in view of the fact that history shows the *first* digit of
past program cost estimates to have been in error, on the average, by
about 100 percent! The General Accounting Office, in its most recent
report on the topic, for example, states that for the Department of
Defense acquisition programs now underway, 67 percent are already
overrun by more than 100 percent (including the effects of inflation).

In the case of the F-18 program it was originally stated to the
Congress that the cost would be twelve billion eight hundred seventy-
five *point three* million dollars. A few years later the same report
defined the probable cost as (not altogether inconsistent with the

23

GAO's findings) *twenty-four* billion twenty-three million. . . and (still!) *0.3* million dollars. Perhaps encouragement should be derived simply from the fact that, although the first significant figure did double, it was possible to maintain the last one unchanged. Detailed analyses by the author show that although the initial digit in program cost estimates is virtually never correct, the last digit does prove to be correct ten percent of the time. This is sometimes called Augustine's Final Law.

George Will, speaking of the President's tax bill, describes the application of this technique in the following words; "He pretended the tax bill wasn't really a tax increase — odd, considering it is supposed to siphon in $98.3 billion. (Note the precision - '.3' - from people who have been unable to guess the deficit within forty-billion dollars.)"

Other examples of the preservation of the *last* digit in cost estimating? The Sydney Opera House (to have been built in 6 years but took 16) was to have cost 7.2-million Australian dollars but actually cost 102-million dollars. English taxpayers were to have paid 150-million pounds for the development of the Concorde supersonic transport but eventually were billed 12.20-billion pounds. (Note that an initial estimate ending in "zero" can assure the success of this methodology.) To prove that agony knows no international boundaries, the Bay Area Rapid Transit ("BART") in San Francisco grew from an estimated cost of $0.6 billion to $1.6 billion.

The whole process is something akin to "getting the last word" — in this case, "getting the last digit." But, then, one must start somewhere.

Nonetheless, by examining the data in Figure 4, it is possible to derive the logic which underlies the practice of quoting fundamentally dubious numbers with a very great degree of apparent accuracy. It is seen from the figure that there is indeed a relationship between the number of "significant figures" quoted and the true precision of the data at hand, but this relationship is just the opposite of what one might expect. The Law of Definitive Imprecision, which is based on a substantive collection of data such as that presented in Figure 4, states:

The weaker the data available upon which to base one's position, the greater the precision which should be quoted in order to give that data authenticity.

(LAW NUMBER IV)

The use of the above law is fairly widespread, with one recent

Relationship of Implied Precision to Actual Precision

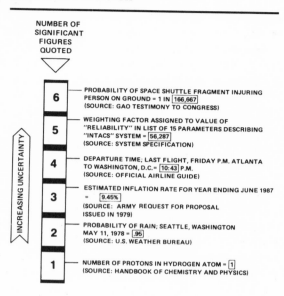

Figure 4   The precision with which any given numerical factor is known should presumably be reflected in the number of significant figures with which it is quoted. This is in practice seldom the case, thereby leading to misinterpretation of the confidence which is assignable to data.

example being the Army Development and Readiness Command's official estimate of the inflation index which will prevail for procurement in the 16th year from the time of the estimate (i.e., in 1995). This index has been stated to be 2.6719—an amazing feat of prescience, particularly in view of the Office of Management and Budget's near-simultaneous adjustment of the inflation rate for the next 12 months by about 3 percentage points!

Similar confidence in projecting future threats is reflected in a document released during 1980 with the marking prominently displayed on its cover, "Declassified on *10 January* 2000." But, fortunately, as Will Rogers reminded, "Numbers don't mean nothin'. It's people that count."

An example from the civilian sector is the U.S. Trust Company's announcement that there are 574,342 people in the United States with assets worth $1 million or more. One cannot help but wonder how such an assessment could be made; or how the marginal qualifiers fared in the hour-by-hour vagaries of the stock market; or if one of them might not have dropped a few grand at the race track and failed to have promptly informed the U. S. Trust Company. Or how the U. S. Census Bureau knows that "in 1980 the U. S. labor force consisted of exactly 104,449,817 workers"; particularly when most employers don't have any idea how many of their own employees are actually workers. It may be that this is all simply a consequence of more widespread use in financial circles than had heretofore been realized of O'Brien's Principle, also called the $357.73 theory, which states, "Auditors always reject any expense account with a bottom line divisible by 5 or 10."

A problem which has long been faced in applying Law Number IV, however, has been what to do in those cases wherein the analyses from which the numbers were derived provide only rather discrete results, such as $1 billion, or 10 miles, or 1 ton. The solution to this dilemma has been astutely derived by Lieutenant General Glenn A. Kent (USAF, Ret.) in his reviews of a large number of quantitative analyses. The solution is quite simple: it consists of simply converting all data from the English system of measures into the metric system and back again!

A derivative of this English-to-metric technique wherein 39.4 inches equates to one meter accounts for such phenomenal accuracies as are identified in a bulletin recently carried in the U. S. from a European wire service concerning a citizen whose private airplane was reported to have missed crashing into the control tower at an airport in Europe "by less than 39.4 inches."

That such undeserved precision can be hazardous, particularly when combined with a law later to be promulgated concerning the unreliability of electronics, is made abundantly clear in the following excerpt from a news article carried by the *Associated Press* regarding "a fuel shortage which caused a Boeing 767 to make an emergency landing. . .The plane, with 61 passengers and a crew of eight, went into a powerless glide from 39,930 feet to a bumpy landing on a Gimli, Manitoba airstrip... Airline workers had resorted to a manual fueling procedure when an electronic system on the aircraft. . .failed. The fuel in the craft is measured in centimeters and converted to liters before departure. That figure is converted to pounds and then to kilograms so that the pilot can calculate the flight plan. It was during this procedure that the error was made, the airline spokesman said."

A related approach appears to have been used in testimony

provided to the Congress by the General Accounting Office in which it was stated that the chances of a person on the ground being injured by a falling piece of a Space Shuttle launched in a northerly direction from Kennedy Space Center "are 1 in 166,667." It may or may not be coincidence that 1 chance in 166,667 equates almost precisely to 6 divided into a million. But clearly, one would not feel nearly as safe knowing that the chances of being hit on the head by a falling piece of the Space Shuttle are about "half a dozen in a million" as he feels when the probability of that happening is a single chance in *one hundred sixty-six thousand six hundred sixty-seven.*

In the same vein of reporting the uncertain with great certainty, the Associated Press released the following story rife with precision concerning the impending crash of the Soviet Cosmos 1902 satellite: "Pentagon tracking experts said later in the day that the satellite. . .would re-enter the atmosphere between 4:45 a.m. MST Sunday and 6:17 a.m. MST Monday. . ." Then in a burst of candor the AP continued, ". . .with Sunday evening the most likely time."

NASA itself apparently embraces the use of such precision, reporting to the press after the first Shuttle launch that the fuel consumed cost "approximately $72,936.90." Not to be outdone, the National Football League tells us that the average weight of its players is exactly 221.84 pounds, and the Federal Education Data Acquisition Council estimates that "9,495,967 man-hours will be spent filling out forms" in a given year. Clearly, that sort of intolerable situation is much more likely to stir beleaguered citizens into action than if only about 10 million hours were going to be spent.

Still another approach for the creation of exactness underlies the fiscal year 1979 appropriation of $25.418 million for the Navy's Aegis program. Certainly, a great deal of detailed study must have been required to define the program's funding needs with such specificity. But, alas, when scrutinized more closely, it is found that the figure is the result of a compromise brought about by a dispute between the House and Senate whereby a lump sum of $11 million was simply patched on top of the original request by the President for $14.418 million!

For sheer audacity in applying Law IV, not even the GAO, the Defense Department, and the Congress *combined* can rival Sir Arthur Eddington. Eddington begins his scholarly book, *The Philosophy of Physical Science,* with the observation: "I believe there are 15,747,724,136,275,002,577,605,653,961,181,555,468,044,717, 914,527, 116,709,366,231,425,076,185,631,031,296 protons in the universe and the same number of electrons." One can only marvel at the contribution which has been made to scientific knowledge by the digital computer; such a high-confidence analysis would never have been possible with a slide rule.

George Gamow in his book *One, Two, Three. . . Infinity* provided useful advice to those who are infatuated with large numbers:

> There was a young fellow from Trinity
> Who took $\sqrt{\infty}$
> But the number of digits
> Gave him the fidgets;
> He dropped math and took up Divinity.

Actually, Sir Josiah Stamp, Her Majesty's Collector of Inland Revenue, was well on the track of Law Number IV nearly a century ago, except that he applied it only to government and neglected its frequent use by industry, among others. Sir Josiah pointed out, "The Government are [sic] extremely fond of amassing great quantities of statistics. These are raised to the nth degree, the cube roots are extracted, and the results are arranged into elaborate and impressive displays. What must be kept ever in mind, however, is that in every case, the figures are first put down by a village watchman, and he puts down anything he damn well pleases!"

In the vernacular of the modern computer age this is simply and widely known as "GIGO": Garbage in. . .Garbage out. Or even more devastatingly, Garbage in. . .Gospel out.

FYI

We sure liberated the hell out of this place.
An American soldier
World War II

Having found a way to anoint specious numbers with credibility, it is not surprisingly a rather trivial exercise for the leadership of our now burgeoning program to neutralize the written and spoken language as well. In fact, they frequently manage to unravel even the King's English while trumpeting the worth of their projects; or, as the saying in Brooklyn goes, "It was the loudest noise they ever seen."

Most major engineering activities depend on widespread public understanding for their funding or for their social acceptance, if not both. Yet, in spite of the many examples of contributions to mankind made possible through technology, the general public still harbors a considerable skepticism of the net benefit wrought by past technological advances. As a result, budgetary and environmental limitations abound and support for basic research continues to erode in many quarters. The problem is exacerbated by the very language which engineers and managers use to communicate their achievements, a language which appears to be formulated to assure that no information might be transmitted. . . either to the public or, frequently, among themselves.

According to Talleyrand, writing some two-hundred years ago, language was given to man to conceal thought. This would certainly appear to be the case in the 20th Century.

A former Principal Deputy Under Secretary of Defense for Research and Engineering, Gerald Dineen, has met this problem head-on, pointing out that "we go to the Congress and tell them that our WWMCCS has got to have a BMEWS upgrade, our Fuzzy Sevens have to be replaced by PAVE PAWS, we want to keep our PARCS and DEW in operation, we have to harden the NEACP, and we have to improve our MEECN with more TACAMO and begin planning to replace AFSATCOM with Triple-S. . . and then we wonder why no one understands." This language, imbedded within a language, has led some contractors in the Command, Control and "Communications" business to place signs over entrances to their plants saying "C³ spoken here."

The extent of the problem faced by the uninitiated can begin to be appreciated by considering the following excerpt from an Air Force document on the implementation of the new acquisition policy, A-109:

- "The HQ USAF/RD sends the draft MENS through SAF/ALR to OUSDRE for OSAF, OSD, DIA and OJCS staff-level comment."
- "The HQ USAF/RD OPR develops the for-coordination draft MENS and presents the MENS comments and proposed solution approach to the HQ USAF RRG for corporate review in lieu of the underlying SON."

To the unwashed, this might convey a message something like:

- "The blank blank/blank sends the draft blank through blank/blank to blank for blank, blank blank, and blank staff-level comment."
- "The blank blank/blank blank develops the for-coordination draft blank and presents the blank comments and proposed solution approach to the blank blank blank for corporate review in lieu of the underlying blank(s)."

Clearly, having drawn such a blank when dealing with the process of replacing ROC's (Required Operational Capabilities) with MENS (Mission Element Need Statements), GOR's (General Operational Requirements), and SON's (System Operational Needs), one can understand why there are those who have been able to conclude only that somehow SON of MENS must have been GOR'd by a ROC.

Of course, the liberal use of acronyms and other means of obfuscation does have the advantage of making sometimes pedestrian material appear rather erudite in that it becomes more difficult to comprehend. Who, for example, would pay a medical doctor twenty dollars in exchange for his scribbling on a piece of paper "Take two aspirin"? Hence, the practice of writing prescriptions in Latin or, at the very least, using indecipherable handwriting.

A practitioner who, rather than admonishing "Take two aspirin," can prescribe "Take two acetylsalicylic acid" and in addition do so with poor penmanship could very likely qualify as a specialist and thereby command at least forty dollars for the services rendered.

As might be expected, the potential of uncommunicative communication has not gone unnoticed by the government and other large organizations. That most intimidating of all documents, the Federal Income Tax Form 1040, is generously sprinkled with IRA's, HR's, IRS's, U.S.'s, FICA's, RRTA's, R&RP's, EI's, EIC's, ZIP's and

. . .ignominiously. . .something called "WIN's."

This striving to impress is also evidenced above the entrances to public buildings where the inscriptions, presumably for the edification of tourists, are of course offered in Latin. It thus may be that no one really knows what "E PLURIBUS UNUM" really means. . . but no one can question that it is impressive.

Ironically, sometimes *erroneous* use of language can be more informative than the correct. For example, again from Pentagon archives, consider the program manager explaining to a senior review group how he was going to extract his program from the serious technical and schedule morass in which it had become mired. Although his verbiage about having "workarounds" already being implemented (what else!) was impressive, his credibility was mortally damaged by his viewgraph - on which the typist had erroneously listed the solution as a "wordaround." In another actual case, the preface to a contractor's proposal to perform a rather exotic technology research project contained a typographical error such that the firm centered its credentials on "a long history of successful participation in *erotic* projects."

A few years ago when in the midst of the national anti-ballistic missile debate the name of the then-troubled Zeus missile was changed to SPARTAN, it was only a matter of hours until some knowing wag had posted a sign on a Pentagon bulletin board proclaiming: "SPARTAN: Special Political Advantages Realized Through Advanced Names." A few years later, the oft-analyzed but never deployed Advanced Manned Strategic Aircaft, AMSA, became known among its much-suffering advocates as "America's Most Studied Aircraft."

Similarly, at a security gate at Cape Kennedy on the approach to one of the launch pads is a sign which, among a number of cautions about explosives, flammable liquids, falling objects, high voltages, etc., conspicuously warns visitors that "POV's are prohibited." Now, this is, of course, cause for consternation among those who may wish to enter but are somehow not exactly certain whether they have a "POV" in their possession. It therefore can be with no inconsiderable relief that one learns that a POV is merely governmentese for a "Personally Owned Vehicle," i.e., presumably a shortened form of the word "car." Correspondingly, a "Range Extension System," better known as an RES in guided bomb parlance, is, in less knowledgeable circles, merely referred to in its short form as a "wing"!

There are those individuals, both outside the government and inside, who are endowed with that special talent to take fairly straightforward concepts and, through suitable embellishment, make

Use of Acronyms in Aiding Communication

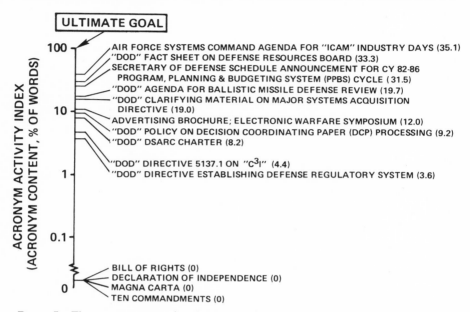

Figure 5 *The excessive use of trade jargon, abbreviations, and acronyms is a major impediment to the communication of ideas.*

them very nearly incomprehensible. The original lucid statement of the acquisition policy which David Packard, then Deputy Secretary of Defense, was to promulgate for the Department of Defense was written by himself and had an acronym content of only 0.2% of the words contained therein. However, by the time this statement was translated by acronymologists, so that it could, presumably, be more readily understood, into the regulation which underpins much of the Defense Department's present acquisition policy (DOD-5000.1), acronyms comprised fully *ten times* the above fraction of all the words in the document. It seems doubtful indeed that Secretary Packard would ever recognize his policy in its new, improved form.

It is suggested that there are those who believe that a measurement of the percent of words in a particular work which takes the form of acronyms can be used to determine the implicit worth of that work. Clearly, the greater the number of acronyms the greater the intellectual value of the material since, obviously, the last thing anyone engaged in communicating would wish to do would be to deny a portion of the audience the message being conveyed. Thus, in view of their widespread use, acronyms must be concluded to be a valuable contributor to the worth of most material.

Figure 5 examines this premise and presents for a number of important acquisition documents the actual acronym use-factor, called the Acronym Activity Index (AAI), measured in the fundamental unit called a "GLOP" (itself not surprisingly an acronym for "Groups of Letters for Obfuscating Points"). The success achieved in the bountiful usage of acronyms in these documents is evident from the enviable ratings shown. These ratings are particularly creditable when contrasted with those of the more acronymically impoverished examples from other writings which are also included at the bottom of the scale. Clearly, communication in the material-acquisition arena has risen to a very high plateau. In fact, a newly prepared government document has a list of 10,000 official abbreviations to be used in specifications alone. Appropriately, the document is referred to as "DOD STD-12."

Law Number V, the Comprehensive Law of Incomprehensibility, derived from evidence such as that just discussed, can be stated:

Profound concepts are often characterized by their difficulty of being understood; therefore persons unfamiliar with Greek or Latin should give intellectual depth to their ideas by utilizing acronyms to a degree more or less proportionate with the lack of sophistication of the ideas being presented. **Q.E.D.**

(LAW NUMBER V)

There are still further advantages to acronymical "anonymity." For example, it may seem quite sensible for a radar designer to point out that HF and UHF are simply too low frequencies to be of much interest for target-tracking applications. However, to state equivalently that "high frequency and ultra-high frequency are too low frequencies to be of much interest for target-tracking applications" would suggest the speaker must be suffering from some form of semantic delerium. Such is the advantage of being obscure clearly.

The current trend toward ever-greater proliferation of acronyms does, however, introduce a spectre of danger: the potential advent of an *Acronym Gap*.

The Defense Marketing Survey has stated that in carrying out its services it has compiled a list of over one million acronyms which are in common usage in defense matters. These consist principally of "words" made up of five or fewer letters. Since the number of possible five-letter (or less) acronyms that can be formed with the English alphabet is no more than about 14 million, it can be seen that nearly ten percent of all possible reasonable acronyms have already been used up. With the accelerating use of such nomenclature, the day when the creation of new systems will no longer be possible thus may not be too distant. This, of course, portends ill since the Soviet Union enjoys a position of inherent acronymical superiority over the U.S. due to its possession of an alphabet containing 32 letters. Some form of accommodation with China and its enormous language population of 14,000 characters would therefore appear to be prudent.

Still another possible solution to the acronymical gap would, of course, be to adopt even longer and less pronounceable letter groupings. . . an arena in which the U.S. Navy has been in the forefront for some time. One necessarily wonders, however, the impact even today on an organization's or individual's self-esteem to be known as the NAVHLTHRSCHEN, the NAVIDISTCOMDTS, COMNAVOCEANCOM or the NAVMEDRSCHU. On the other hand, this identity might not appear all that unattractive to individuals assigned to such organizations* as ARF, ARG, NEMISIS, DRAG, AGED, MORASS or AFWL (pronounced "awful"), but would represent a considerable come-down to the Chief of Naval Air Training, CNATRA, better known simply as "Sinatra."

Many acronyms do not mean what the inexperienced observer might suspect. . . ANTS, GNATS, DOG, FROG, COD, APE, RAT, BAT, RAM and CLAM have nothing whatsoever to do with the animal kingdom or Noah's ark. Rather, they quite clearly stand for Airborne Night Television System, General Noise and Tonal System, Development Objectives Guide, Free-Rocket Over Ground, Carrier On-deck Delivery, Advanced Production Engineering, Ram Air Turbine, Ballistic Aerial Target, Reliability and Maintainability, and Chemical Low Altitude Missile, respectively.**

In the evolution of an acronym, letter combinations which defy pronunciation are simply reconfigured. Thus, National Emergency Airborne Command Post, NEACP, becomes the "Knee Cap"; the Combat Developments Objective Guide becomes the "Sea Dog"; the

---

*Aerospace Recovery Facility, Amphibious Readiness Group, Naval Ship Missile System Engineering Center, (Nuclear) Design Review and Approval Group, Advisory Group on Electronic Devices, Modern Ramjet System Synthesis, Air Force Weapons Laboratory.

**The author experienced the type of problems which can arise from such double meanings on the very first day of a recent tour in the Pentagon. While faithfully carrying out an assigned appointment schedule on Capitol Hill in preparation for a forthcoming confirmation hearing, the author felt it rather inappropriate that typed after the name of several Senators on the calendar was the notation "OLD SOB." It was only some time later that it was learned that "OLD SOB" can, in Washington, also mean "Old Senate Office Building." Nonetheless, the ambiguity, in several instances, lingers to this very day.

Nuclear Weapons Development Guide becomes the "New Dog"; the Airborne Laser Illuminator, Ranger and Tracking System becomes "Alley Rats"; and the Radar Target Scatterer becomes the "Rat Scat." This strange practice by the pursuers of things technological is best explained by the words of Mark Twain: "They spell it Vinci and pronounce it Vinchy; foreigners always spell better than they pronounce."

The next anthropological stage in the development of an acronym takes place when verbal representations of a set of letters are converted back into a written form, a stage in which, inexplicably, the resulting acronym is often totally different from the one which started out! Thus, the Fixed Special Surveillance (radar) known as the FSS-7 becomes, when rewritten, the "Fuzzy Seven." Or the electrical unit, the Pico-Farad, is abbreviated PF, which, after phonetic transliteration, is itself often de-breviated "Puff." The ultimate state of maturity of an acronym occurs when it is finally written in lower case and everyone forgets that it is in fact an acronym. . . such as "radar" and "laser."

Actually, those working on aerospace and other national security matters can make no particular claim to superiority in the acronymical arena. Regulators in all areas have excelled in the exploration of this powerful means of increasing confusion among the unwashed. Consider the world of federal finance, where the unpronounceable "FNMA" simply becomes a Fannie Mae. . . closely related, it is said, to a Freddie Mac. Still other mortgage instruments closely parallel in terminology some of the expressions already discussed pertaining to defense matters, such as SAM's, RAM's, FLIP's and ARM's. Most ominous in the world of mortgages is something called a GPAM, occasionally pronounced "Gyp 'em."

But amid all this confusion is to be found redeeming virtue: countless numbers of Russian cryptanalysts must surely be fruitlessly engaged in trying to understand what American managers are talking about.* Consider, for example, the dilemma of a Russian cryptanalyst confronted with the task of reporting to his superior a passage dealing with topics such as the computer language: "Jules Own Version of the International Algebraic Language, Seismic Intrusion Detection Systems, Clear Air Turbulence, Multiple Independently Targetable Reentry Vehicles, Modular Electronic Warfare Simulators, Modular Electro-optical Warfare Simulators, High Altitude Particle Physics Experiments, Beacon-only Bombing Systems, Development Ob-

---

* Most American engineers speak two foreign languages: FORTRAN and English.

jectives Guides, Surface-to-Air Missile (Systems), Battlefield Area Reconnaissance Systems, Weather Observing and Forecasting Systems, Hostile Weapons Locating Systems, Submarine Anomaly Detection, Tactical Air-defense Computerized Operational Simulators, Biological Aerosol Detection, Automatic Test Equipment, Anti-radiation Missiles, Tables of Organization and Equipment, Mutual Assured Destruction, Built-in Test, Inertial Navigation, High Altitude Transmission Experiment and Directional Attack Mines."

Such a report by a Soviet analyst might sound something like:

JOVIAL SIDS CAT, MIRV, MEWS and MEOWS.
HAPPE BOBS DOG, SAM, BARCS, WOFS AND HOWLS.
SAD SAMS TACOS, BAD MIRV ATE.
MIRVS ARM AND TOE, MAD SAM BIT IN HATE.
. . . DAM!

But as bad as this may be, it *could* have ended with a reference to Effective Radiated Power.

In summary, simply stated, it is sagacious to eschew obfuscation.

Replacing Congress with an Equation

Why rob banks?. . .
That's where the money is.
W. Sutton

In order to survive to completion, every government-sponsored development program must maintain an extremely high single-skirmish-survival probability in its encounters with the various steps in the budget cycle. In the congressional approval process alone, a defense program's budget will be voted upon at least 18 times a year, or a total of 144 times in the average program's lifetime. . . thus the need to keep a program moving rapidly. Managing programs in this environment is much like raising cattle in some of the more barren areas in Texas where a cow is said to have to graze at 60 miles per hour just to stay alive. Fortunately, the project in question had been designed with just this in mind, and careful recognition given to the need each year to extract the requisite funding from the duly anointed sources. The budget preparation process was itself proceeding normally, with each organizational layer deleting the favorite projects of the layer immediately above it, in hopes of forcing add-on's of funds as the senior managers scrambled to save their own favorites — a practice commonly called "gold-watching." The fundamental viability of this tactic is, of course, dependent upon unsuspecting compliance by the next-higher management layer;a condition made difficult by the fact that the next-higher management layer is itself simultaneously identifying the gold watches it will be using to circumvent its next-higher layer. Meanwhile, the staff in the Senate is making preparations to double the requested funds for the program, whatever they might be, so as to be able to reach a suitable compromise (as has been occurring for many years) with the House of Representatives. . . which will in turn be halving the budget request on this program.

Former Deputy Secretary of Defense Frank Carlucci was once asked how he could tell, when he moved on to another in the long

37

Predicting Congressional Changes to the Defense Budget Request

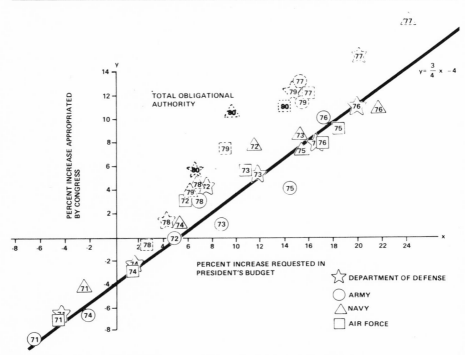

Figure 6 The aggregate impact of the Congress in the budget process is quite predictable, although gradual shifts do take place over time.

series of high-level government posts he has held, who were the constituent pressure groups and what were their objectives. His answer: "No problem. The constituent groups will find you and will be quite vociferous in what they want. And 98 percent of the time, whether it's poor people or defense manufacturers, the issue is money, and their position is that they want some of it."

It does not seem to be possible to determine a priori the probability that any particular program will be funded or terminated by the Congress in any given year. It is, however, possible to predict with very good accuracy what the overall impact of the congressional approval process will be on the defense budget. That is, the result, in the aggregate, of the yearly congressional review process can be reduced to a simple equation.

Figure 6 displays the effect of congressional actions on the Administration's defense budget requests in each year of the present decade. It is seen that a trend line can be quite accurately drawn which will predict the outcome of the congressional review process on the budget of any given military department, or on the Department of Defense as a whole. This would suggest that the Administration's efforts to gain approval of its budget requests have about the same impact year after year, independent of the political parties involved or the magnitude of the budget change requested, the latter even over quite large excursions.

These observations are summarized in the Uniform Law of Infernal Revenue:

In any given year, the Congress will appropriate for defense the amount of funding approved the prior year plus three-fourths of whatever change the Administration requests, minus a 4-percent tax.*

(LAW NUMBER VI)

This law has accurately applied over a range of year-to-year changes in the requested funding level extending from minus 7 percent to plus 24 percent.

Apparently disappointed with its demonstrated record in shaping overall budgets, the Congress, undaunted, seems to have determined to move into new arenas. . .such as design engineering. For example, in the case of the small ICBM program, for which the payload and range are relatively invariant, the House of Representatives took it upon itself to legislate the weight of the missile as 3300 pounds. How the legal precedence of this law ranks with those of Newton, Kepler and Euler remains, presumably, to be determined by the truly *Supreme* court.

If nothing else, the well-established engineering management milestone, the CDR (Contract Design Review), may take on an altogether new meaning. . .and become a *Congressional* Design Review.

---

*Data for years subsequent to the original formulation of this Law (1971) would suggest that as concern increased over the growth in Soviet military capability in the latter part of the decade the tax was gradually eliminated.

Courtesy of Englehard from Monkmeyer.

Chapter 2

Minor Oversights

Marginal Costs

The winning contractor, safe in the knowledge that superior ability had once again prevailed, and the losing contractor, reassured once again political influence had snatched defeat from the jaws of victory, turned their attention to the tasks at hand:seeking changes to the contract and preparing a protest, respectively. Only slightly exhausted from the requisite series of victory parties, the winning contractor also begins work in earnest on the project. The pace is intense. The marketing group is doubled in size and its leader promoted in recognition of the success which the program will undoubtedly enjoy. The contracts group, numbed by the euphoria of newly discovered power, makes only minor note of the fact that the initial funding may have to be curtailed due to a government budget reduction, which in turn was necessitated to fund the overrun on some other less well conceived and managed program. And the engineers all disappear into their laboratories to start changing their design.

Lord Kelvin once observed that "Large increases in cost with questionable increases in performance can be tolerated only for race horses and fancy women."

It therefore appears worthwhile to examine in some detail the proposition that "the best is the enemy of the good" — a precept which has had its heritage variously traced to the Russians, the Chinese and the Arabs. Whatever its origin, there is considerable modern evidence to attest to its endurance. That is not to say that in terms of personal and organizational attainment there can ever be any goal other than to be "the best." The problem arises when this latter perspective is applied to that old bugaboo. . .hardware.

In times of rapidly advancing technology, by waiting until tomorrow to begin a project it will always be possible to incorporate a little more advanced technology and presumably to make the item being sought still a little bit "better." But come tomorrow, there will be yet another carrot just over the horizon. Thus, the surest way to get nothing is to insist on waiting for everything. In the military sphere, for some years now the Russians have been fielding large quantities of equipment viewed by Western technologists with some condescension, presumably because it is clearly inferior. . . to that which we do not yet have.

The requirements generation process, the method by which the capabilities of future systems are determined in the U.S., basically consists of enthusiastic engineers in industry promising to deliver "all the capability you want for a dollar" and a customer which generally responds, "I'll take two dollars worth." It seems that some people just won't take "yes" for an answer. The dilemma is worsened by the fact that the customer's "requirements" are frequently viewed as sacrosanct even though initiative and imagination are, of course, always highly encouraged in responding to the government's needs. Experience has shown, however, that winning contractors can bid anything they want. . .as long as it is what the government wanted in the first place.

Congresswoman Pat Schroeder, speaking at a House Armed Services subcommittee hearing, expressed her exasperation at the inability to make difficult choices and thereby eliminate costs in the following terms: "If those guys were women, they'd all be pregnant... they can't say no to anything!"

The temptation to flirt with the edge of the state of the art does appear irresistible to many, yet often results in the would-be developers finding themselves in circumstances wherein they are ill-equipped to work their way out of problems and then must face a very skeptical Congress listening to their excuses. It is much as if these technological explorers were following the course of an inmate at the Butte County Jail in California, who explained his brief absence from the jail to skeptical sheriff's deputies in the following manner, as reported by a national wire-service: "I was playing pole vault and I got too close to the wall and I fell over the wall. When I regained my senses I ran around to try and find a way back in, but being unfamiliar with the area, got lost. Next thing I knew I was in Chico." Clearly this gentleman must have been an R&D manager in some earlier incarnation.

Not only does operation near the edge of the state of the art often greatly increase cost and risk, but in addition it can have a seriously deleterious effect on reliability. One might ask Mario Andretti for his views on this subject, in recognition of his being intimately familiar with the process of squeezing the last ounce of performance from high-technology machines; specifically, the Indianapolis Formula One auto racer. Andretti's record over the years gives insight into the hazards of operation near the edge of the state of the art, particularly, once again, when it is not altogether clear which side of the edge one is on. The evidence:

MARIO ANDRETTI'S "INDIANAPOLIS 500" EXPERIENCE

YEAR	PERCENT OF RACE COMPLETED	OUTCOME
1965	100	Finished third
1966	14	Engine exploded
1967	29	Lost wheel
1968	1	Burned piston
	(42)	(Replaced another driver, burned piston again)
1969	100	Won race
1970	99	Engine smoked
1971	6	Crashed into wall
1972	97	Ran out of gas
1973	2	Burned piston
1974	1	Broken piston
1975	25	Crashed into wall
1976	51	Engine smoked
1977	—	Did not race
1978	93	Oil leak
1979	—	Did not race
1980	36	Engine seized
1981	100	Finished second
1982	0	Crashed at start
1983	42	Crashed

Even when dealing with *available* technology, the best is often inordinately expensive. Sometimes this cost is, of course, very worthwhile in that it provides the winning margin — that narrow edge between victory and defeat. But other times, particularly in times of fixed overall budgets, the practice of seeking that last little bit of capability can be not only very costly but also very counterproductive. In the case of aerospace projects, it is all too common. . .as more and more capability is demanded and less and less weight margin survives . . .to end up with a machine on whose behalf engineers can claim little more than that perhaps it is held together by "structural paint."

Consider the matter of seeking to increase reliability through redundancy. . . a policy often employed, and appropriately so in most cases. But when the part most likely to fail is also the dominant cost contributor, this practice serves as a convenient example of the high price of improving a system's capability. For instance, increasing the reliability of an element with an *inherent* reliability of 80 percent by just 16 more percentage points will double its cost if achieved through duplication. The next 3 percent will *triple* the cost. . . and so on.

That this phenomenon is not unique to reliability is shown in Figure 7, which presents the cost of obtaining ever-increasing performance for items ranging from optical components to baseball players. The difference in market price between a .250 hitter and a .300 hitter is marked. . . even though the actual performance difference is merely that one will get a hit just one more time then the other every twenty

The High Cost of a Little More

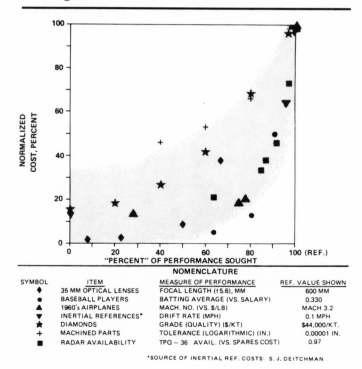

SYMBOL	ITEM	MEASURE OF PERFORMANCE	REF. VALUE SHOWN
♦	35 MM OPTICAL LENSES	FOCAL LENGTH (f 5.6), MM	600 MM
●	BASEBALL PLAYERS	BATTING AVERAGE (VS. SALARY)	0.330
▲	1960's AIRPLANES	MACH. NO. (VS. $/LB)	MACH 3.2
▼	INERTIAL REFERENCES*	DRIFT RATE (MPH)	0.1 MPH
★	DIAMONDS	GRADE (QUALITY) ($/KT)	$44,000/KT.
+	MACHINED PARTS	TOLERANCE (LOGARITHMIC) (IN.)	0.00001 IN.
■	RADAR AVAILABILITY	TPQ – 36 AVAIL. (VS. SPARES COST)	0.97

*SOURCE OF INERTIAL REF. COSTS: S. J. DEITCHMAN

Figure 7   A disproportionate share of the cost of most purchases is concentrated in a very small fraction of the features sought. So-called "extras" are particularly flagrant contributors to cost in both the commercial and government marketplaces.

tries. Similarly, the price of a normal investment grade diamond jumps from $6,800 per karat to $44,000 per karat when the demand is made that it be flawless (Grade D). Much the same is true of airplanes, inertial reference systems, etc.*

That "nice to have" features can be costly is certified in the answer of a recent million-dollar-lottery winner to a question about what he had done with all the money. His answer: "To be honest, I spent half of it on liquor, gambling, and women. The rest I wasted."

Once features are designed into a system they are very, very difficult to remove. Bert Fowler, while serving as Deputy Director of Defense Research and Engineering, observed that one can plot the increase in cost of a system *versus* its total capability as each successive feature is added. The "Fowler Hysteresis Law" states, "When each element of capability is successfully subtracted until a system's capability is altogether gone, 30 percent of the cost still remains!".

These observations comprise the foundation for the Law of Insatiable Appetites, which traces its origin to automobile salesmen and their omnipresent "extras," and may be stated as follows:

The last 10 percent of the performance sought generates one-third of the cost and two-thirds of the problems.

(LAW NUMBER VII)

The price of the ultimate is very high indeed. Sometimes it would seem one might be better served by having more of a little less. If not, the penultimate outcome seems to be to have nothing, albeit of the *very* highest capability.

The secret, if there is one, to controlling the costs which are added by the pursuit of peripheral albeit impressive capabilities is actually quite straightforward and can be seen in the workings of a sculptor creating a statue of a hippopotamus. How does one make a statue of a hippopotamus? Very easily; one obtains a large block of granite and chips away every piece that does not look like a hippopotamus.

---

*In the case of inertial reference unit precision, smaller is better. To accommodate this the available data were spread across the ordinate of the plot in linear fashion. The grade of diamonds has been treated in the same manner, a practice which probably understates the cost of increasing quality.

Costing Enough To Be Useful

*Live within your income
even if you have to borrow to do it.*
Josh Billings

*Among the minor items which have been neglected in our
program as it builds momentum is the fact that, promising
as the project is, it will in the day of reckoning be forced to
fit within a budget which is long on demands by other
programs. . . and short on funds. Law Number VIII explains the empirically observed relationship between the
cost of an item and the quantity of that item which is
purchased; or, as tennis pro Ilie Nastase noted in explaining
his failure to report the loss of his wife's credit card,
"Whoever has it is spending less than she was." But in the
excitement attendant to our accelerating program this is no
time to be concerned with the remote possibility that the
planned procurement of a large quantity of hardware might
somehow be affected by the fact that each individual item is
admittedly quite costly. This project will most assuredly be
different. What you see is what you get, and no one who
saw the proposal could doubt that a lot was to be got.*

Figure 8 shows the rather unexpected relationship which exists
between the quantity of an item which is purchased and the cost per
unit of that item. It is seen that most articles fall along a constant trend
line which encompasses equipment spanning from the $100 per copy
LAW antitank rocket to the multibillion dollar aircraft carrier, Nimitz.
Why this should be the case may help explain some underlying difficulties in the material acquisition process.

One obvious explanation is that the quantity of an item which can
be afforded depends on the cost of the item, and the number
procured is a simple consequence of that one fact. This seems to be a
rather unsatisfactory interpretation, however, since it implies that
there are no *unique requirements* for larger or smaller quantities of
various types of equipment; one merely buys few of an item because it
happens to be more costly or many because it happens to be less
costly, independent of what the item may be intended to do or of the
need for that item.

In this regard it is interesting to note that there exists a maximum
acceptable unit price, $10^{10}/N^{1.2}$, for *any* individual item of equipment

50

Cost-Quality Tradeoffs in Military Hardware

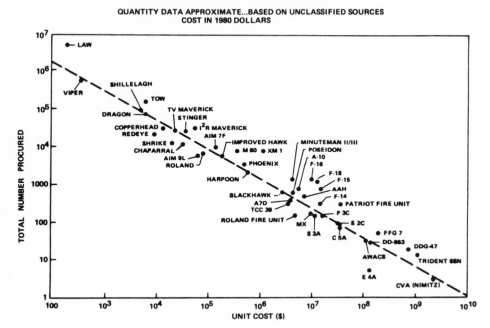

QUANTITY DATA APPROXIMATE...BASED ON UNCLASSIFIED SOURCES
COST IN 1980 DOLLARS

Figure 8   As the unit cost of an item increases the quantity of that item which is likely to be purchased, not surprisingly, decreases. What is perhaps surprising is the predictability of this falloff.

and this price depends only on the quantity, N, of that item which is to be purchased. Once the quantity has been determined, the striking conclusion is that the cost of all items gravitates to this maximum. Additional capabilities somehow creep into the hardware until the unit cost approximates the above-mentioned value, which is know as the Threshold of Intolerance. Merely putting the word "strategic" in front of the name of a program will, for example, instantly double its cost.

Thus, any item of which only a few are needed can (and will) be allowed to take on additional features until the unit cost rises to the vicinity of the limit described. Bert Fowler, Vice President of the MITRE Corporation and former Deputy Director of Defense Research and Engineering, has pointed out that for some reason a mess table on a nuclear submarine costs substantially more than a mess table on a conventional submarine. Similarly, a clock in a Mercedes Benz costs a great deal more than a clock in a Volkswagen. So it goes with each component until the capability and cost of the entire system rise to the

Threshold of Intolerance as described in the Law of Conservation of Input:

The features incorporated into any system will continue to increase until the unit cost of the system in dollars approximates the Threshold of Intolerance, which is defined as $10^{10}/N^{1.2}$, where N is the quantity of the item which is to be purchased.

(LAW NUMBER VIII)

This trend toward higher cost is, of course, exacerbated by the fact that the exponent in the denominator above is greater than unity. This means that the high unit cost which is acceptable for low-quantity items more than offsets the volume impact of high-quantity items. . . so that a contractor does slightly more business by dealing in high-cost/low-volume materiel. Similarly, program managers of high-unit-cost items will be able to enjoy the status of directing larger overall enterprises than their counterparts dealing in more economical systems, albeit procured in larger volume.

On the other hand, an approximation to Law VIII is that the quantity of an item procured multiplied by its unit cost always equals 10^{10} dollars. This provides a convenient method of determining the total procurement quantity for most programs.

Over the years others have studied various effects related to the one noted herein. Dr. Al Flax, President of the Institute for Defense Analyses and former Assistant Secretary of the Air Force, has pointed out one such interesting investigation described in the 1939 edition of *Airplane Design*. In that book, K. D. Wood addresses the relationship between the quantity of various types of aircraft which were purchased and the price of those aircraft. A principal difference in the observations of Professor Wood and the present data is, sadly, that the most expensive aircraft in the former study cost less than $5,000!

In those early days, however, the pressure toward more capable and more costly designs was already at work. Professor Wood notes in passing that "the Curtis-Wright, Jr. airplane was designed to the following simple specifications, listed in order of importance: (1) low first cost, (2) safety, (3) appearance and performance." Professor Wood goes on to explain that "the actual first cost achieved in building this airplane (about $1400 retail in 1930) was considered at the time to be exceptionally low, though the safety record was not quite so satisfactory, and the sacrifice of performance (cruising speed of about 65 mph) turned out to be so excessive that the airplane found little use as a means of transportation in competition with the automobile."

The seeds of increasing expectations were sown at an early time.

The High Cost of Buying

*The winning contractor's demeanor could not help but
remind an observer of that exhibited by the dog which
actually caught the car. Among the minor annoyances
which had somehow been overlooked in the now
burgeoning program was the prospect that warfare may,
fortuitously, be pricing itself out of existence. The price of
the project had become so enormous that its continued
viability was in grave doubt. But this is no time to raise
questions about fundamental matters; certainly not in the
formative stages of a project.*

It can be shown that the unit cost of military equipment, as is the
case with much other high-technology hardware, is increasing at an
exponential rate with time. Figure 9 shows, for example, the historical
trend of rising unit cost in the case of tactical aircraft. From the days of
the Wright Brothers' airplane to the era of modern high-performance
fighter aircraft, the cost of an individual aircraft has unwaveringly
grown by six db per decade . . . a factor of four every ten years. This
rate of growth seems to be an inherent characteristic of such systems,
with the unit cost being most closely correlated with the passage of
time rather than with changes in maneuverability, speed, weight, or
other technical parameters. The same inexorable trend is shown in
Figures 10 through 13 to apply to commercial aircraft, helicopters, and
even ships and tanks, although in the last two *somewhat* less
technologically sophisticated instances, the rate of growth is a factor of
two every ten years.

The cost of high-technology military hardware can then be accurately explained in terms of an increase by a factor of four during
each sunspot cycle, independent of anything else.

The significance of this observation does not, however, lie in the
mere fact that cost growth is, in itself, predictable. Rather, it lies in a
comparison of the rate of growth of, say, aircraft unit cost with the rate
of growth of other seemingly relevant parameters. . . such as, say, the
defense budget. This particular comparison is presented in Figure 14,
wherein the identical data points shown in Figure 9 pertaining to the

Trend of Increasing Cost of Tactical Aircraft

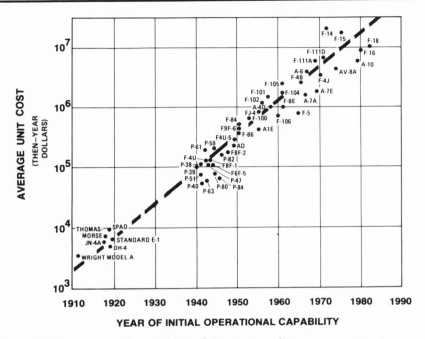

Figure 9   The unit cost of tactical aircraft has increased in a very consistent manner ever since the beginning of the aviation age. The rate-of-climb is a factor of four every ten years.

cost of aircraft are reproduced, but to a smaller scale in order to facilitate extrapolation into the future. Objection might be raised as to the validity of any such extrapolation; however, it is noted that the above-mentioned trend has faithfully prevailed throughout the entire history of aviation, presumably making such extrapolation no more hazardous than the common practice among economic forecasters in Washington of extrapolating based on a *single* data point.

When the trend curves for the national budget for defense and the unit cost of tactical aircraft are, in fact, extended forward in time, as shown in Figure 14, a rather significant event can be predicted for the not-too-distant future: namely, the curves *intersect*. And they intersect within the lifetimes of people living today. This observation has led to the formulation of what is known in some circles as the First Law of Impending Doom and in other circles as the Final Law of Economic Disarmament:

Trend of Increasing Cost of Commercial Airliners

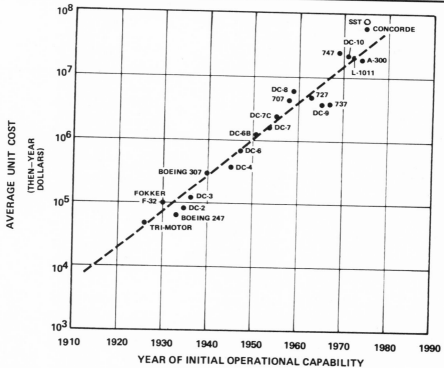

Figure 10   *The trend of increasing cost with time has been basically the same for commercial and military aircraft. In both cases major performance advancements have been achieved . . . but not without cost.*

In the year 2054, the entire defense budget will purchase just one tactical aircraft. This aircraft will have to be shared by the Air Force and Navy 3 1/2 days each per week except for leap year, when it will be made available to the Marines for the extra day.

(LAW NUMBER IX)

One can only imagine the difficulties that such an arrangement will entail. There will be, for example, the advocates of rotary-wing aircraft who will point to the corresponding plot for their devices, noting with pride that due to successes in cost control a "fleet" of *rotary-wing* aircraft would not dwindle to the quintessential machine until the year 2064. Just what happens in the decades *after* the year 2054 or 2064

Trend of Increasing Cost of Helicopters

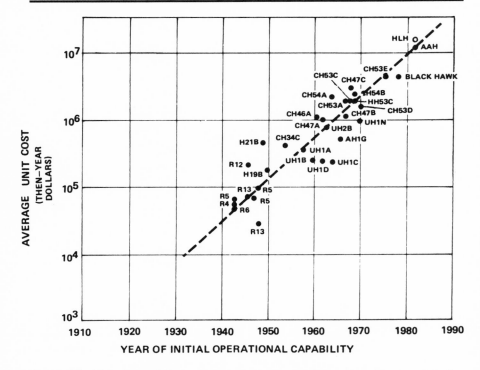

Figure 11   The slope of the unit cost vs. time curve for rotary-wing aircraft is the same as for fixed- wing aircraft, albeit getting off to a somewhat belated start.

is not altogether clear, but it is believed to have something to do with the now officially recognized and widely touted "stealth aircraft," whose presence must be taken on faith since it alledgedly cannot be seen.

It should be pointed out to those who take solace in challenging the validity of the above extrapolation of the defense budget that, were a plot of the gross national product to have been used instead, the aforementioned singular event would have been delayed a mere 60 years. In this latter era the cost of aircraft will no longer be measured in dollars but a new unit will be introduced, the "GNP," pronounced "nip." Hence, an aircraft in the year 2100 will cost about half a nip.

Dr. John Wall has pointed out that this law demonstrates that "all the military might of the U.S. will be concentrated into one grand vehicle in the latter half of the 21st Century. But this is just the Battlestar Gallactica which we all know so well. . . with perhaps a few

Trend of Increasing Cost of Aircraft Carriers

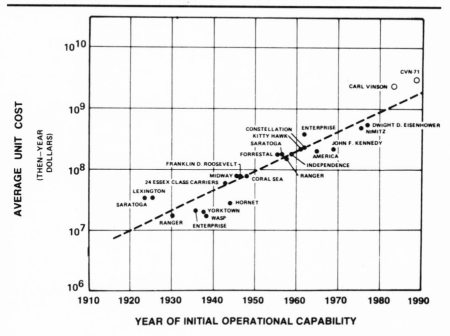

Figure 12   Aircraft carriers, now costing about $3 billion each with their complement of aircraft, exhibit a rate of cost increase about half that of the aircraft themselves.

smaller ships such as the USS Enterprise preceding it by 50 years or so. And in the mid-22nd Century we find: Darth Vadar's planet-size Death Star! One single grand fighting machine encompassing a whole nation—or perhaps a whole planet!" Seldom has the power of extrapolation been so majestically stated!

This particular law might, perhaps, more accurately be remembered as "Calvin Coolidge's Revenge" as a tribute to the prescience of that gentleman with regard to matters aeronautical. It will, of course, be recalled that it was Calvin Coolidge who in 1928 asked, in a moment of budgetary frustration over paying $25,000 for a *squadron* of aircraft, "Why can't we buy just one aeroplane and let the aviators take turns flying it?" Calvin Coolidge was ahead of his time.

Turning to the commercial arena, such has been the pace of progress in aeronautics that the seats in a modern jetliner cost more than a twin engine airliner of the late 1940's. In fact, a modern airliner costs five times the market value of the entire airline industry as it

58

Trend of Increasing Cost of Tanks

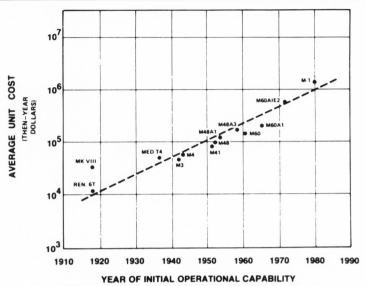

Figure 13   Tanks, as well as other fighting vehicles, obey the same historical cost trends as aircraft and ships, evidencing a rate of increase more closely matching the latter.

Calvin Coolidge's Revenge

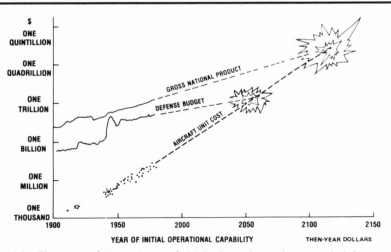

Figure 14   The cost of tactical aircraft built throughout the recorded history of aviation, as represented by the dots, can be accurately projected in a manner which points to a singular problem in the not-too-distant future.

Trend of Increasing Cost of Bomber Aircraft

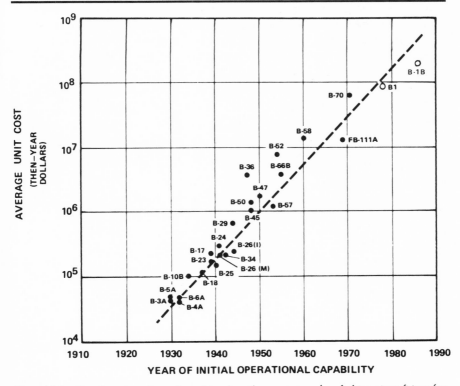

Figure 15   Bomber aircraft are found to obey the same trend as fighter aircraft insofar as generation-to-generation cost increases are concerned. The higher absolute value of these costs, however, has subjected bombers to more intense politico-economic warfare than fighters.

existed in 1938. But a daring extrapolation of the spectacular growth rate in airline passenger-miles flown (5 percent increase per year) and of the US population growth (1.4 percent per annum) leads to the astonishing conclusion that in a mere 250 years it will be necessary for the *entire* citizenry of the United States to be airborne *24 hours a day, every day*. Although this will unarguably reduce freeway congestion, the concept of a nation's populace continually flying around with an airplane of some sort strapped to its posterior somehow seems extraordinarily unbecoming.

Figure 15 shows the corresponding trend in unit cost of bomber aircraft, culminating in the B-1 phantom data point. For the sake of consistency, this curve can be referred to as "Jimmy Carter's

Revenge" or Ronald Reagan's Derevenge." But in spite of the fact that as a flying project the B-1 seems to have left more people disgruntled than gruntled, it nonetheless serves as a powerful example of the use of this particular law.

Simply waiting for things to settle down to abnormal just doesn't seem to be working in this case.

But somewhere lurking in the background there remains the echo of that troublesome warning by Lenin: "Quantity has a quality all it own." American technologists, in their more optimistic moments, sometimes refer to this asymmetry as possessing a "target-rich" battlefield. . .an expression which may trace its origin to General Custer.

Wait 'Til Last Year

*I was shipwrecked
before I got aboard.*

Epistles 87,1

The fact that the operational inventory was drifting inexorably toward that single, all-consuming, aircraft did little to dissuade the program's participants from designing into their newest product a veritable cornucopia of exotic features. That this could be safely done was attested by the government's official five-year plan, which showed striking growth in the size of the operational inventory. Furthermore, this projection was not simply a temporary figment of some forecaster's inexperience — the same projection had been holding solid for a number of years. Only the start-point for the soon-to-be realized recovery had been changing. . .slipping at the rate of about one year per year.

As the old vaudeville line goes, "They told me to cheer up... things could be worse; so I cheered up and, sure enough, things got worse." Consider, for example, the number of combatant ships in the U.S. Navy. For a number of years projections have been made recognizing that budgetary austerity would force a near-term decline in the number of ships in the fleet. These projections, however, always predicted that the longer term would see a strong recovery. As shown in Figure 16, this projection has proven to be fully half-correct:the number of ships has declined in the near-term as projected but in the real world longer-term, sure enough, things *also* got worse.

In the words of Quintus Ennius some twenty-two centuries ago, presumably concerned over the future of the Roman fleet, "No one regards what is before his feet;we all gaze at the stars."

In fact, it seems to have been characteristic for centuries for planners to stumble over their feet as they gazed into the distance. A potpurri of historical examples, borrowed from the eminently qualified, is offered for the humility of all would-be prognosticators.

- "We must not be misled to our own detriment to assume that the untried machine can displace the proved and tried horse."
  Maj. Gen. John K. Herr, 1938

- "As far as sinking a ship with a bomb is concerned, it just can't be done."

  RADM Clark Woodward, 1939

- "The popular mind often pictures gigantic flying machines speeding across the Atlantic carrying innumerable passengers in a way analogous to our modern steam ships. . . . it seems safe to say that such ideas are wholly visionary and even if the machine could get across with one or two passengers, the expense would be prohibitive to any but the capitalist who could use his own yacht."

  William H. Pickering, Astronomer, 1910

- "The [flying] machines will eventually be fast; they will be used in sport but they should not be thought of as commercial carriers."

  Octave Chanute, 1910

- "Aircraft flight is impossible."

  Lord Kelvin

- "While theoretically and technically television may be feasible, commercially and financially I consider it an impossibility, a development of which we need waste little time dreaming."

  Lee DeForest, 1926

- "Just as certain as death, [George] Westinghouse will kill a customer within six months after he puts in a system of any size."

  Thomas Edison

- "The energy produced by the breaking down of the atom is a very poor kind of thing. Anyone who expects a source of power from the transformation of these atoms is talking moonshine."

  Ernest Rutherford

- "Railroad carriages are pulled at the enormous speed of 15 mph by engines which, in addition to endangering life and limb of passengers, roar and snort their way through the countryside, setting fire to the crops, scaring the livestock, and frightening women and children. The Almighty certainly never intended that people should travel at such breakneck speed."

  Martin Van Buren

- "Aerial flight is one of that class of problems with which man will never be able to cope."

  Simon Newcomb (1903)

- "We hope the professor from Clark College [Robert H. Goddard] is only professing to be ignorant of elementary physics if he thinks that a rocket can work in a vacuum."

  Editorial, New York Times, 1920

- "There has been a great deal said about a 3,000 mile rocket. In my opinion such a thing is impossible for many years. I think we can leave that out of our thinking."

  Vannevar Bush, 1945

- (On the occasion of the dedication of a physics laboratory in Chicago, noting that the more important physical laws had all been discovered): "Our future discoveries must be looked for in the sixth decimal place."

  A. A. Michelson, 1894

- "By no possibility can carriage of freight or passengers through mid-air compete with their carriage on the earth's surface. The field for aerial navigation is then limited to military use and for sporting purposes. The former is doubtful, the latter is fairly certain."

  Hugh Dryden, 1908

- "Fooling around with alternating currents is just a waste of time. Nobody will use it, ever. It's too dangerous. . . it could kill a man as quick as a bolt of lightning. Direct current is safe."

  Thomas Edison

- "I can accept the theory of relativity as little as I can accept the existence of atoms and other such dogmas."

  Ernst Mach (1838-1916)

- "Rail travel at high speeds is not possible because passengers, unable to breathe, would die of asphyxia."

  Dr. Dionysys Lardner (1793-1859)

- "What, Sir, would you make a ship sail against the wind and currents by lighting a bonfire under her deck? I pray you excuse me. I have no time to listen to such nonsense."
  Napoleon to Robert Fulton

- "That is the biggest fool thing we have ever done. . . the [atomic] bomb will never go off, and I speak as an expert in explosives."
  Adm. William Leahy to President Truman, 1945

- "Space travel is utter bilge."
  Sir Richard van der Riet Wooley, The Astronomer Royal, 1956

- "There is no hope for the fanciful idea of reaching the moon, because of insurmountable barriers to escaping earth's gravity."
  Dr. F. R. Moulton, Astronomer, University of Chicago, 1932

- "X-rays are a hoax."
  Lord Kelvin

It *is* difficult to prognosticate, as the saying goes, *especially* about the future.

That larger inventories of ships, as well as aircraft and tanks, are probably justified based on the increases evidenced in like Soviet equipment over the past two decades is not at issue. The problem is that continual "get-well-fast" forecasts are *actually believed*. . .not only by those who *do* the forecasting, but also by corporate marketing managers. This same phenomenon has been attributed by some to the sales forecasts of the Edsel and the Concorde, to select just two examples from the commercial world.

Thomas Jefferson explained this tendency of planners to view the world through rose-colored glasses in the following words: "I like the dreams of the future better than the history of the past."

In this environment, large numbers of new projects are started, betting that funds will be available to complete them in the good times, which must assuredly lie ahead. The difficulty is that the good times that lie ahead always seem to do exactly that:lie ahead. A tortuous cycle then begins wherein many projects are begun; inadequate funds are subsequently available to conduct them as planned; in order to avoid the obvious waste of cancelling programs in which substantial investments have been sunk, all programs are stretched; these stretchouts increase costs; the increased costs exacerbate funding shortfalls; further stretchouts are then required; and so on *ad destructum*.

The F-15 aircraft experienced exactly such a course when un-projected budgetary limitations precluded the planned production rate. A substantial number of aircraft which were to have been built during a peak production period had to be pushed downstream and patched onto the end of the production line some three years later. The result was that, although the total number of aircraft to be purchased remained constant at 729, the cost of these same aircraft increased by nearly two-billion dollars. These additional funds could have been used to purchase an additional wing of 72 aircraft had in fact fewer other programs been begun and the original, more-efficient production plan used.

When looking at forecasts such as those shown in Figure 16, there seems to be a convoluted belief that what goes down must come up; or, as the old adage states, the grass is always greener on the other side of the mountain. Erma Bombeck has made the more modern observation that the grass is always greener over the septic tank. . .and we indeed seem to be existing, insofar as Figure 16 is concerned, in the pits.

Reality Sinks In

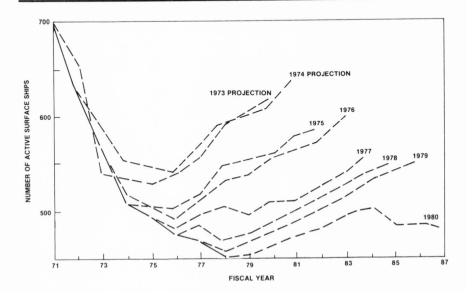

Figure 16 For many years official projections have shown an eventual increase in the size of the fleet. For many years this has not been happening.

Unfortunately, or fortunately, this problem is not peculiar to the planning of any particular commodity or even of any particular nation: Witness the Soviet economic five-year plans. As in the U.S., everything is always projected to recover fully within the next five years. What may, in fact, be needed is a *one-year* plan; for then forecasters almost certainly would project complete recovery in just one year and we wouldn't have to wait so long to find out we are in trouble.

All of which leads to the pragmatic Law of Surrealistic Planning:

If today were half as good as tomorrow, it would still be twice as good as yesterday.

(LAW NUMBER X)

But at least most planners are consistent. Consistently wrong.

The Reliability of Unreliability

Adde parvum parvo magnus acervus erit. *
Ovid

The technological sophistication and indeed the high cost of the product entering development almost certainly assure that it will be highly effective and highly reliable. Scant attention thus need be afforded to the law which deals with the relationship between the reliability of complex hardware and that human tendency reflected in the World War II placebo: "We know of not a single instance wherein the enemy has successfully used camouflage against us." However, with respect to the matter of enhanching reliability, we have in fact viewed the enemy; and, to once again quote that immortal possum, "He is us."

It does appear to be fundamental to the human race to believe that which one wants to believe rather than that which a logical examination of fact would reveal. Francis Bacon says that "man prefers to believe that which he prefers to be true." George Santayana puts it in the following terms: "All living souls welcome what they are ready to cope with; all else they ignore or pronounce to be monstrous and wrong. . . or deny to be possible." It would appear that Mark Twain may have been unduly generous toward humanity when he speculated, "I believe that our Heavenly Father invented man because he was disappointed in the monkey."

Consider the crucial matter of producing more reliable hardware; in particular, electronic hardware, which everyone knows is comprised of components whose individual reliabilities have been improving at a rate of about 15 to 20 percent per year for nearly two decades. Further, with size decreasing dramatically and the aggregate cost of integrated circuits consistently decreasing since 1963 along a 75 percent learning curve, it should be possible to achieve extraordinary system reliability through careful component selection and built-in redundancy. . . and thus to eliminate what has been one of the most troublesome problems for electronic equipment users for many years: *unreliability*.

---

*"Add little to little and there will be a big pile." Quoted from *The Mythical Man Month*, by Frederick P. Brooks, Jr.

In the words of Lieutenant General Orwin Talbott, "The longer a man is in a command position on the battlefield, the less enamored he is of the technological edge and the more obsessed he becomes with trying to make what he has work."

Now, if one were not privy to the anachronistic behavior of engineering and management activities as they have been dissected herein, one might in fact unwittingly conclude that as more and more money is spent on an item, its reliability would get progressively better and better. The initiated would never fall into such a logical trap and would recognize immediately that quite the opposite must be true. That this latter situation indeed prevails is verified in Figure 17 which exhibits field reliability data on a number of airborne electronic systems as collected during the Electronics-X study conducted under the aegis of the Institute for Defense Analyses. It is seen that the items examined range from relatively simple devices, such as marker beacons and glide-slope indicators, to completely automated multichannel airborne intercept systems. The costs and reliability factors change with increases in inflation and technology. . . but the

Impact of Increasing Unit Cost on Field Reliability

Airborne Electronics Equipment

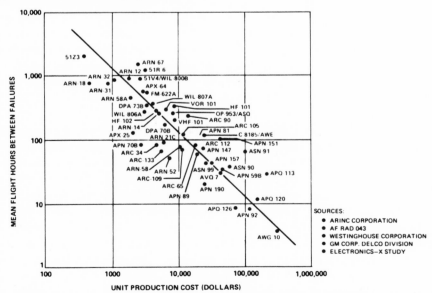

Figure 17   The more an item of electronics costs the less reliable it is likely to be. As successive generations of technology evolve, the overall reliabilty curve shifts parallel to its predecessor, but the trend of decreasing reliability with increasing cost tends to remain inviolate.

trend at any given time remains unwavering. Whatever the spectrum of equipment and techniques involved, the conclusion is unmistakable: as cost increases, reliability does not improve; rather, it worsens. Frank McKinney Hubbard (1868-1930) advised, "If at first you do succeed, quit trying." This is summarized in the Law of Undiminished Expectations:

It is very expensive to achieve high degrees of unreliability. It is not uncommon to increase the cost of an item by a factor of ten for each factor of ten degradation accomplished.

(LAW NUMBER XI)

Dr. Eb Rechtin, President of The Aerospace Corporation, points out that such has been the pace of technological progress that by spending $250M for an item, a mean time between failures of 30 seconds can be guaranteed. Correspondingly, one might suspect that a mean time to repair of 30 months could be suffered.

Although great care must, of course, be taken in interpreting the meaning of a "failure" (all failures are not created equally, nor do they have equal consequences), data released on the mean flight hours between failure for twelve different types of Navy and Air Force fighter and attack aircraft are illuminating. Nine of the twelve aircraft experienced a "failure" at least once every 30 minutes. Of those, five experienced failures every 15-20 minutes. This would seem to be conclusive proof of the correctness of those who have argued that the next strategic bomber must be supersonic rather than subsonic.

In any event, it can be understood why there are those who argue that an airplane is merely a collection of spare parts flying in close formation.

It should be noted that the above law, regrettably, cannot be limited solely to airborne electronics. For example, even that most "ground-borne" item of military hardware, the tank, is a notorious offender. The M60A2, the first tank having an all-electric turret control system, contained 35,000 parts in the turret alone (and in the field performed for many years exactly like a tank with 35,000 parts in the turret alone). It was, in fact, just such a design which once caused Dr. John Foster, then the Director of Defense Research and Engineering, in an understandable moment of pique, to answer a question as to how one might best defeat a tank assault by saying, "Give them plenty of room to run around and they will all break down!" When considering the enormous logistical burden created by such problems of unreliability, some solace can perhaps be derived from the realization that if the Soviet Union's tanks have no better reliability and repair rates than ours, then with their huge inventory the Russians are stuck with more broken tanks at any given moment than we own *altogether*.

What, of course, is happening is that as component reliability improves, *more components* are crammed into each system to provide more and more capability—that is, more capability during those interludes wherein the system is not broken. A modern jetliner has about 4.5 million parts including 100 miles of wiring. The Nike Hercules air defense system contained well over one million parts. But if a system has one-million single-string parts, each with a reliability of 99.9999 percent for performing some specified mission, the overall probability of the mission *failing* is over 60 percent. The foreman of a tank plant perceptively explained the solution in the following terms: "The part you engineers don't put on the machine ain't going to cause no trouble."

Even such an unsophisticated element as a solder joint can become a source of major problems when, as for example in the case of the Patriot air-defense unit, there are two million of them.

Thomas Paine summed it all up in the 1790's when he counseled, "The more simple anything is, the less liable it is to be disordered, and the easier repaired when disordered." Sadly, it has become commonplace to view high technology and simplicity as contradictory terms. The two are not, in fact if not in practice, antonyms. The problem is to use technology in a fashion which engenders simplicity. Who could argue, for example, that today's pocket calculators are less reliable than their 18,000 vacuum tube predecessor, the ENIAC, which completely filled a room in the 1940's?

Law Number XI, which states that *expensive* systems won't work, can be seen to pose a particularly serious dilemma to equipment designers when it is applied in conjunction with Law Number XXVI, which will note that *inexpensive* systems are *not possible* (they require infinite testing). This may all be academic, however, since it has also been established (in Law Number IX) that before long it will not be possible to afford any new systems anyway.

A Long Day's Night

A knife without a blade,
for which the handle is missing.

Lichtenberg
18th Century

It had admittedly been demoralizing to learn that all the money being poured into their product was merely guaranteeing that it wouldn't work. But the bad news was yet to come. This latter news had to do with maintenance of broken machines; but fortunately, this particular problem could be deferred because of management's foresight in previously eliminating all maintenance planning activity from the budget. This had occurred during the funding cuts which were needed to make the animated movie to show customers how well the system was going to work. Unfortunately, not inconsiderable embarrassment and controversy surrounded even this seemingly innocuous filmmaking venture when the corporate P.R. department erroneously registered the movie with the Library of Congress under the category reserved for "Science Fiction," a particularly grievous error in that it diverted attention from the fine job the corporation's President had done in narrating the widely distributed film.

For many years a great deal of discussion has been devoted to the matter of building equipment which can be easily maintained, and in particular maintained by individuals with only limited time in which to master their sometimes demanding calling. For example, a decade ago attentive visitors to one of the major control centers for the defense of North America would have observed, hanging inconspicuously from the door knob of a giant room literally packed with the most advanced electronics, a small tag noting reassuringly, "All equipment in this room has been checked and OK'd by Private First Class Smith."

Actually, considerable time and effort have been devoted in industry as well as in the government to preparing maintenance plans, spares plans, fault isolation plans, training plans, and the like. The problem is that, in the stampede to give this area greater and earlier attention in a program, most of the plans have suffered from a minor

72

oversight: they were constructed *long* before anyone knew what the actual hardware was going to comprise. Similarly, dozens of reliability analysts were placed diligently at work multiplying long strings of nines (reliability analysts need only learn to work with nines), but their usually encouraging results seldom had any resemblance to the failures which ultimately produced the disasters. These latter events were instead the consequences of a bracket rubbing on a wire until it broke, a seal installed upside down, a leaky valve, an overheated resistor, a cold solder joint, or an improperly torqued nut.

Worse yet, so powerful became the cult of the "ilities" (reliability, maintainability, availability. . .) and their incessant awareness campaigns that attention was actually *diverted* from the real task of designing and building high quality hardware. The ultimate consequence was that in more than one company large but carefully isolated groups were established offline simply to make the posters and fill in the ponderous forms demanded by their compatriots in the "ilities" in the government*. . . but to do so in a manner which would divert interference from those charged with actually designing the hardware. Thus, the *critically* important matter of assuring maintainability became, in the real world, even more peripheral.

It should not be surprising then that the removable panels on one aircraft required nine *different kinds* of fasteners to be released before access could be gained. . . or that the parts which most often broke were the ones that were buried the deepest inside the machine, always carfully located adjacent to the sharpest and hottest component to be found. Or that, as was often the case, nonstandard, peculiar wrenches, bolt threads, washers, and wire gages were called out in maintenance manuals, which themselves always related to the previously phased-out model. One Army maintenance manual advised the mechanic in effect that all he had to do was "remove the center nut and accompanying washer affixing the left anchor bracket (when viewed from the right side of the platform looking toward the forward panel) by turning the nut in a counter-clockwise direction with a standard socket wrench, using extreme caution not to interfere with the high voltage electrical power supply immediately to the left and below the adjacent connector and harness."

So much for the volunteer Army. It may be safer to be an infantryman than a mechanic.

Worse yet, it has all too often been found that, when a trained mechanic was available who in fact possessed the mind of an Einstein,

*The Law of the Request for Proposal: "A career in every paragraph."

The Price of High Cost

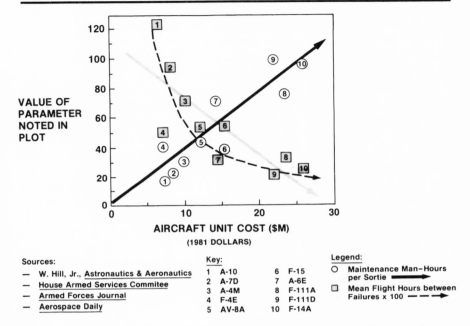

Sources:
— W. Hill, Jr., Astronautics & Aeronautics
— House Armed Services Commitee
— Armed Forces Journal
— Aerospace Daily

Key:
1 A-10   6 F-15
2 A-7D   7 A-6E
3 A-4M   8 F-111A
4 F-4E   9 F-111D
5 AV-8A   10 F-14A

Legend:
○ Maintenance Man–Hours per Sortie ➤
▢ Mean Flight Hours between Failures x 100 — — ➤

*Figure 18 More costly, and therefore usually more complex, hardware is charac-
terized by increasing maintenance demands. This need not be the case. It merely is.*

the dexterity of a surgeon, and the agility of a chimney-sweep, the
needed replacement parts were not available. Even a systems analyst
would be able to understand that it makes little sense to buy twice as
many airplanes only to have three-fourths of the total grounded for
the lack of spare parts. In the spares business, as in personal finance,
there always seems to be too much month left over at the end of the
money.

But this is not a case of bad news and good news. This is a case of
bad news and worse news. It may in fact be true that, as more and
more money is spent on an item of hardware, the more often it
breaks; but it is also true that the more one spends for an item of
hardware the more maintenance hours will be required to try to keep
it fixed. This is illustrated in Figure 18 wherein it is observed that as
investment cost goes up the mean-time-between-failures drops; but at
least the maintenance manhours go up! This is, presumably, good
news only from the standpoint of some day assuring zero unemployment. Some of the new aircraft now entering the inventory will,
we may hope, reverse this trend. . . Time will tell.

The real difficulty stems from the fact that, as has already been noted, the parts which break are, by the well-established natural law discussed earlier, always the ones located in the most inaccessible places. Therefore, only a few mechanics are able to crowd around them simultaneously, an observation which may seem elementary but which in fact will be seen to have dire consequences.

Consider the matter of maintaining a modern high-performance airplane, an airplane which in most instances will have been designed to fly *at least* one sortie each day. The difficulty which arises is that, as suggested in the figure, when more and more money is spent on an aircraft, eventually the sum of the required maintenance *crew* hours plus flight hours *will exceed 24 hours each day!*

In view of the well-established impossibility of reducing maintenance demands by virtue of reducing the *cost* of airplanes, some other more realistic solution must be sought to negate this dilemma. Setting aside such expediencies as developing a breed of miniature mechanics or adopting in-flight maintenance (similar to in-flight refueling but using accompanying airborne garages instead of just filling stations)* the most promising solution seems to reside in the Augustine-Morrison** Law of Unidirectional Flight:

> **Aircraft flight in the 21st century will always be in a westerly direction, preferably supersonic, to provide the additional hours needed each day to maintain all the broken parts.**
>
> **(LAW NUMBER XII)**

Horace Greely was insightful.

---

* The space program, it should be noted, has already adopted the concept of spaceborne garages — as for example the use of the Shuttle to rendezvous with the ailing Solar Max spacecraft so that an astronaut can replace a fuse!
** James B. Morrison, Operations Intern, Martin Marietta Aerospace.

Malice in Wonderland

But Benjamin's mess was five
times so much as any of theirs.
Book of Genesis

The program appears to be completely under control. The overrun is now increasing at a decreasing rate and the contractor is losing money less rapidly than at any time in its history. Euphoria prevails. But before closing the second act in the story of our program's life it seems worthwhile to examine the personnel management system which underpins its very existence. Law Number XIII examines the incentive system. . .and demonstrates that managers who produce exceptional results can expect the rewards they receive to be increased. Unless, of course, they stay the same or go down.

"Call it what you will, incentives are the only way to make people work harder." The words of Andrew Carnegie? The creed of John D. Rockefeller? Or perhaps of Henry Ford? No, as it happens, these are the words of none other than that old capitalist Nikita Kruschev speaking on the benefits of the incentive system.

Having thus established the manner in which incentives are viewed in the Soviet Union, it is instructive to examine their use in the system extant in the United States, for which incentives form the very foundation: the Free Enterprise System.

Figure 19 displays the ranking of the 50 most profitable firms in the United States in 1978 as compared with the rank according to pay received of the individuals who led those companies the prior four years.*

The following law, known as the Augustine-Dozier** Law of Distributive Rewards, explains the evidence in Figure 19 (with apologies to P. K. Wrigley of baseball fame):

There are many highly successful organizations in the United States. There are also many highly paid executives. The policy is not to intermingle the two.

(LAW NUMBER XIII)

---

*For the occasional instances where the leadership changed during the period examined, the data for that company are not included in the figure.

**Susan Dozier, Operations Intern, Martin Marietta Aerospace.

Relationship of Executive Wages to Company Performance

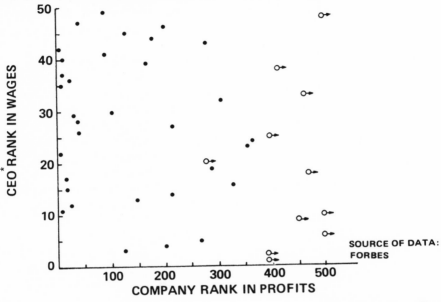

WAGE RANKINGS BASED ON 1978 DATA
PROFIT RANKING BASED ON PRIOR 4–YEAR AVERAGE

*Chief Executive Officer

Figure 19 *It is difficult to detect any relationship between the wages of key executives and the performance of the firms they lead.*

If a plot is made showing rankings according to return on equity, the *lack* of correlation exhibited is even more striking than that found in Figure 19 for absolute profits. The evidence seems to be incontrovertible: The Bottom Line is alive and well — but it just doesn't seem to be of much interest in terms of rewards and incentives.

Samuel Goldwyn appears to have been only half correct when he observed, "We're overpaying him but he's worth it."

Further, although one could never confuse the operation of the US government with the Free Enterprise System, it is still striking that an overt effort at demotivation has been practiced whereby the top five layers of management have on occasion all been fixed at the identical pay level due to the imposition of an apparently arbitrary wage ceiling.

General Dave Jones, Chairman of the Joint Chiefs of Staff, describes the implications of these management practices by drawing the following fascinating view of the Joint Chiefs' organization (Board) as it would appear through the eyes of an industrialist:

Board consists of five directors, all insiders, four of whom simultaneously head line divisions . . . reports to [both] the chief executive and a cabinet member . . . supported by a corporate staff which draws all its officers from line divisions and turns over about every two years . . . line divisions control officer assignments and advancement; there is no transfer of officers among line divisions . . . Board meets three times a week to address operational as well as policy matters, which normally are first reviewed by a four-layered committee system involving full participation of division staffs from the start. . . at seventy-five percent of the Board meetings, one or more of the directors are represented by substitutes . . . if the Board can't reach unanimous agreement on an issue, it must—by law—inform its superiors . . . at least the four top leadership and management levels within the corporation receive the same basic compensation, set by two [congressional] committees consisting of a total of 535 members . . . and any personnel changes in the top three levels (about 150 positions) must be approved in advance by one of the committees.

It is eloquent testimony to the talent of individuals involved that many of our institutions have been made to work at all.

Courtesy of *Phoenix Gazzette*.

Chapter 3

The Gathering Storm

Piled High

You know, I think you and I have some of the same people working for each other.
**Nikita Khruschev to Allen Dulles, Director of CIA,
at State Department Reception**

Although it must unfortunately be reported that a few alarmists are beginning to appear, the task of establishing a design and management structure for the program are moving ahead unimpeded. Focus is still being placed on the need to find a suitable position for all those in the government and the contractor's organization who were so instrumental in obtaining approval of the project in the first place. But this proves not to be a difficult task, although it is admittedly somewhat complicated by the need simultaneously to absorb the management of a sister program inexplicably terminated due to some problems which arose with cost, schedule, and performance.

Professor C. Northcote Parkinson would not be disappointed were he to apply his studies, which revealed a growing shore contingent in the British Navy in spite of a steadily decreasing number of ships at sea, to U.S. management practices now. The present law expands modestly on Parkinson's work so as to examine the *organizational* or *structural* consequences of operating with heavily peopled administrative overheads. As Czar Alexander put it, "I did not rule Russia; ten-thousand clerks ruled Russia."

That the extent of an administrative structure is still relatively insensitive to the amount of work to be performed is reaffirmed in Figure 20, which presents one piece of the available evidence — in this case, the agricultural industry. That the same is true of the aerospace industry is asserted by Kelly Johnson, former Director of Lockheed's renowned Skunk Works, who pointed out to the Senate Committee on Armed Services, "I have made constant surveys over the 20 years about what percentage of an engineering group actually is engaged in putting a line on paper, writing an analysis that has to do with the hardware. . . . I found that 5.6 percent of the total time was spent in actually addressing the problem: how to make the hardware. I found out about 10 years later they were down to 3 percent."

In a related vein, Dr. Bob Frosch, former NASA Administrator, during a talk on "Bureaucratic Engineering" wondered how, when he

Independence of Size of Administrative Layers to Size of Work Force (a la Parkinson)

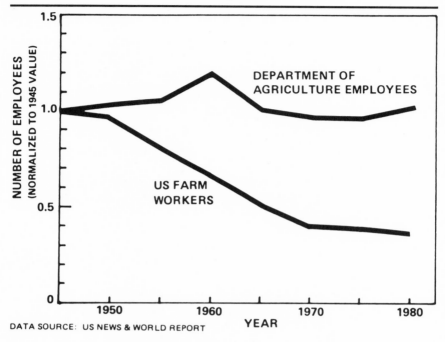

DATA SOURCE: US NEWS & WORLD REPORT

Figure 20   As the number of individuals involved in "touch-labor" decreases, the size of the supporting (overhead) labor pool expands to take up any slack.

divided the cost per engineering manyear into the annual budget to build some small item, the hordes of engineers that seemed to result were ever going to manage to crowd around the lonely piece of hardware that was being constructed. His conclusion was, "From time to time I have been able to identify and demonstrate in a particular case that about one-tenth of the engineers involved were in fact doing engineering in any traditional sense and the rest were writing each other memos."

The problem with the existence of large bodies of administrators is not merely a consequence of their number, *per se*, but rather is a result of the number of *layers* they constitute. . . with each *layer* having an opportunity to reject, deny, modify, eliminate, reduce, stretch, or otherwise retard every suggestion that has the audacity to seek to wind its way through the labyrinth-like approval process which would have made even a Minotaur proud. Each layer thus functions much as a delay line in a radar set. Unlike professional football, however, there is no penalty in U.S. management practices for "piling-on." The General Accounting Office, for example, reports that the Mark 48 torpedo project was led by 87 subordinate program managers.

Although widely recognized, solutions to this problem have been inhibited by the fact that where managers stand depends on where they sit. It has been pointed out by Dr. Paul Berenson, Executive Secretary of the Defense Science Board, that management is what one does to provide sound leadership of those below one's self on the organization chart. On the other hand, he says, micromanagement is all that which takes place above one's self on the chart.

An individual working at the bottom level at the Army's Missile Command is looking up at 44 layers through which must be gained support for any new idea before it can be funded. The view from such a valley must be demoralizing indeed. As one Canadian flatlander was observed to remark, "Mountains are OK, I guess, but they sure do get in the way of the scenery."

The statistical implications of the above assessment are devastating. Consider the probability of obtaining approval of a project which must be agreed upon by 40 different layers, each of which has almost a 99 percent likelihood of reaching an affirmative decision. As shown in Figure 21, despite the favorable individual odds, the chances of overall success in such a case are only about fifty-fifty. This is pointed out by Robert Massey's Law which, slightly paraphrased, notes that one vice-president, two vice-admirals and three GS-18's wired in series produce near infinite impedance. *The Washington Post* refers to the progenitors of this impedance as "The Abominable No Men."

Examples in the figure for specific organizations count "deputies" as a "layer" as well as counting staff levels as layers. On the other hand, they neglect altogether the existence of multiple parallel channels in the approval process at any given layer which must also somehow be hurdled. Further, for many actions, such as budget approvals, it is necessary to penetrate this thicket not once, but once each year. There are said to be some alive today who believe it may be possible to get to heaven without going through Atlanta; but there can be none who would suspect that one can get funding without passing through each and every passageway of the approval maze.

One Air Force general has defined a "yes" as being "the requisite ninety-nine non-no's." Dave Packard, a former Deputy Secretary of Defense and currently chairman of the Board of Hewlett-Packard Company, cites the example of the Argon National Laboratory in Chicago. He notes "that nineteen separate congressional committees act on line items before Argon's budget can be approved."

84

Idea Survivability

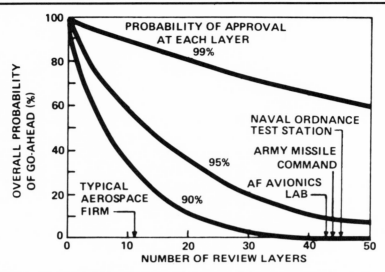

Figure 21   The probability of successfully accomplishing any objective declines in a very calculable manner as the number of layers in the approval process increases.

But all this merely addresses the *Federal* Government, itself simply the end in a system shown to encompass 81,000 local governments, 3,000 counties, 18,000 cities and villages, 17,000 townships, 25,000 school districts, and 18,000 special districts.

But in all these organizations rare indeed is the individual who can go do something or make something happen. Rather, the situation is as described long ago by Samuel Johnson. "To do nothing is in every man's power."

Actually, the probability of peeling one's way through the onion-like layers of the approval process without obtaining a "no" somewhere along the way may be the *least* threatening aspect of the system. But there is a "Catch 22," the implications of which can be illustrated by a few simple back-of-the "request-for-approval" calculations.

Data presented by Col. G. D. Brabson, for instance, reveals that prior to seeking program approval from the Defense System Acquisition Review Council (a committee established to streamline the decision process), the program manager of the Patriot Air Defense system was required to present no fewer than 40 briefings to intervening layers so that they could approve what he was going to say when he arrived at the pinnacle of the streamlined management system. In the case of the Joint Tactical Information Distribution

System (JTIDS), 42 separate appearances were required not including Saturday matinees. The F-16 aircraft necessitated 56 of these prebriefings, whereas the F-18, a best-seller, enjoyed 72. These data equate to 53 briefings on the average passage.

Now, since there are typically 18 layers (Service Material Command, Service Staff, Service Secretariat, Office of Secretary of Defense staff, each with its own strata) between a program manager and the DSARC members, it can be readily determined (invoking Law Number IV) that par is 2.944 briefings per layer.

Consider an individual at the very *bottom* layer who happens to have an idea, the pursuit of which requires annual budget approval. This individual must pass through at least 42 layers with an impedance of 2.944 BPL (briefings per layer). Under the modest assumption that each briefing consumes two days for preparation, travel, presentation, and recuperation, the total approval cycle occupies 250 days. . .which is exactly the number of working days in a year! When you are wrestling a gorilla, YOU rest when the *gorilla* wants to rest.

And none of the above accounts for the special demands that take effect when any out-of-the-ordinary needs arise. For example, when the managers of the B-1B and F-16 programs sought approval from the Congress for multiyear funding, about 100 special briefings were required of each program.

Thus ends the mystery of why new ideas seldom manage to bubble forth from the system designed to encourage creativity.

The DSARC forum was of course established to permit "face-to-face streamlined decision-making" among high-level officials. Records of the GLCM (Ground Launched Cruise Missile) program reveal that the average dry-run of a DSARC program was attended by fully 24 individuals. Thus, recalling the average of 53 briefings *prior* to a DSARC, we have a total attendance at these intimate management gatherings of 1,272. . .rivaling some of the crowds drawn at other sporting events in Washington.

Further, according to official records, even after a DSARC meeting is completed, it takes an average of 27 workdays to sort out what has been concluded with sufficient accuracy that it can be documented. Columbus would never have made it through a DSARC. And even if he had, the General Accounting Office (GAO) would have excoriated him. Not only did he not know where he was going, but when he got there he didn't even know where he was. He would be a cinch for the Golden Fleece award.

Stratification also introduces profound problems in the realm of titular engineering and heraldry. . . an area where the U.S. has only recently been able to challenge its European allies or, for that matter, the Soviet Union. This has led, for example, to the creation in the U.S. of such positions as the one listed in the telephone book for the Department of State's Agency for International Development as the "Associate Assistant Administrator in the office of the Assistant Administrator for Administration." Similarly, when it was decided that the Under Secretary of Defense for Research and Engineering, who already had a layer of deputies who themselves possessed a sublayer of assistants who were in turn buttressed by deputy assistants, sensed the need for still another layer, the rank of *Principal* Deputy Under Secretary was created. When it was subsequently found that not one but *two* such individuals were needed, the system took right in stride the creation of *two Principal* Deputy Under Secretaries for Defense Research and Engineering!

The Law of Propagation of Misery summarizes the above treatise on organizational layering and is fairly easily derived from the data presented in Figure 21:

If a sufficient number of management layers are superimposed on top of each other, it can be assured that disaster is not left to chance.

(LAW NUMBER XIV)

If Noah were alive today he would find no need to construct an ark; he would need only create a management structure of the above type and assign it responsibility for making rain.

What Goes Up. . . Stays Up

You canna expect
to be baith grand and comfortable.
James Matthew Barrie, 1891

The situation had become so perilous that the headquarters even established an internal review to see if a staff reduction at the headquarters itself might be possible. In one subsequent instance the reviewers found two of their colleagues, occupying a near-empty office, who, when asked what they did, answered, "Nothing; absolutely nothing." Responding to the gravity of the situation, the reviewers reluctantly concluded that one of the two should be discharged. A cartoonist in a business magazine recently depicted two executives, in the presumably humorous but not particularly flattering caricature often reserved especially for businessmen, viewing a chart which displayed a plummeting sales trend. The caption has one of the beleaguered executives exclaiming excitedly, "What do you mean cut the fat? We are the fat!" Every new program, of course, needs a large number of support functions to help those who must do the work get their work done efficiently. Also, it is necessary that the members of both the work group and the support group be undistracted by emotional or physical discomforts. The bottom line of such considerations has come to be known as "overhead," and when suggestions are solicited for its reduction the sound of the silence is generally deafening.

There are probably few areas of management more challenging to engage or more fundamentally cantankerous than that of controlling overhead. . . and particularly so because there are few areas wherein managers at all levels can be claimed to be so literally a part of the problem—or, as it is sometimes called in moments of descriptive candor, "The Burden." A still better description was that used by Bill Carlson in his days with TRW: "The real problem is not overhead," he said, "what is really stifling is the underfoot."

It is, of course, a widely accepted tenet of business economics that in hard times overhead rates tend to creep upward; this is logically explained by the need to spread fixed costs over a smaller base,

Effect of Industry Sales Base on Overhead Rate

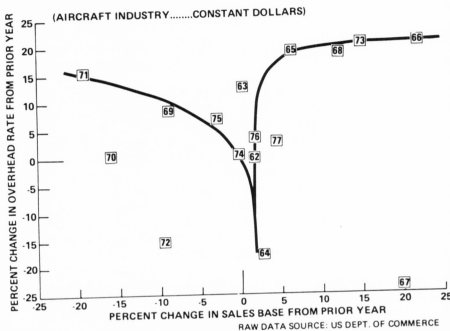

Figure 22 *Although the data relating overhead costs to business volume are varied, there is little evidence to support the conventional wisdom that increased base begets reduced overhead.*

exacerbated by less efficient production rates and the need for increased research and marketing to help reverse the downward sales trend. Managers therefore happily anticipate the day of an increasing sales base when the opposite will be true and overhead rates will properly and automatically reduce themselves.

Figure 22 addresses this matter based on industry-wide overhead rates collected for the aerospace segment by the Department of Commerce. The figure clearly confirms that in times of decreasing base, overheads do indeed increase. But, alas, it additionally confirms, as is widely suspected by most modern-day practicing Don Quixote's of management who have jousted with overhead rates, that in prosperous times overhead rates also tend to increase. Through some sneak-circuit of nature, overheads, software, entropy, and laws all seem to share a common property. . .they increase.

Figure 23 shows that the most visible element of overheads—fringe benefits—themselves abide by the same trend. When business goes

The Impact of Sales Changes on Fringes

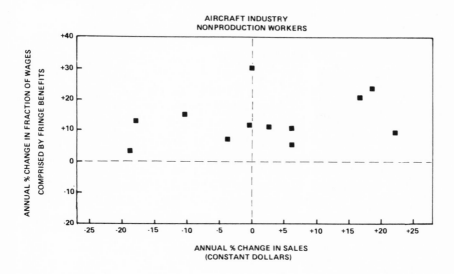

DATA SOURCES: DEPT OF COMMERCE
AEROSPACE INDUSTRY ASSN
(1968-1978)

Figure 23   The persistent growth in fringe benefits is an increasingly important element of overhead costs and often has proved to be quite resillient to changes in business conditions.

down, fringes go up. When business goes up, fringes go up. . . *even when stated as a fraction of total costs of wages.* Thus, for example, the Department of Commerce reports that in the turbulent years from 1968-1980, fringes steadily increased as a fraction of total cost of wages from 10 percent to 46 percent for nonproduction workers in the aircraft industry, and from 14 to 66 percent for production workers.

To quote the most dreaded words among the professional marketeering community, "He took me for lunch."

When it comes to overheads, there is no such thing as bad times: all times are good. . . although, as seen from the figure, some may be gooder than others. At least as viewed from one perspective.

Several years ago, a newly elected executive of a large corporate conglomerate was making his initial visit to a steel mill which had just come under his jurisdiction. Having observed several times during the course of the day one worker slowly running a small hand-file over a huge steel billet, the executive finally overcame his reluctance to exhibit his lack of knowledge of the steel business and inquired of the worker what he was making. The answer came back as straight-forwardly as could ever be hoped: "Six dollars and eighty cents an hour. Why?"

Addressing the loss of U.S. jobs to foreign competition, due in part to high overheads and in part to inefficiency, James Baker of General Electric outlines our future choices in very straightforward terms: (1) automate, (2) emigrate, or (3) evaporate.

Tantalizingly, the data points in Figure 22 indicate one exception to the rule wherein overhead went down as base went up; however, this unusual instance unfortunately seems to be exactly that—an unusual instance: a forerunner to almost nothing. The particular fairing of a trend curve through the data shown in the figure could certainly be argued, but, sadly, no one could ever confuse the data as supporting the conventional wisdom of an overhead rate inversely proportional to sales base. One possible solution to this dilemma is to be found in Wilder Bancroft's 1931 article in *The Journal of Physical Chemistry*. In this scholarly treatise, Bancroft points out that disagreements between theoretical and experimental results can generally be resolved if one multiplies the experimental findings by a factor equal to the ratio of the theoretical expectation to the experimental measurement. However, seeking, at least for the moment, some other approach, it is instructive to examine the expanding universe theory as it applies to the dynamics of overheads.

Hardly a manager is alive today who has not in fact experienced surprise and puzzlement at finding overhead rates rising, contrary to all expectations and diligent efforts, during a period of "good times." Perhaps such a period is simply aptly named. It is much as if the established laws of economics have been repealed. . .hurtling us toward the zenith of a policy that may have been espoused prophetically by one recent administration: "Zero *Base* Budgeting." And, to the eternal frustration of managers who seek to put major overhead reductions into effect, the major impact of their actions is usually no more than to set into motion once again what has historically come to be known as "The Great Timecard Hunt."

This same phenomenon is familiar to any design engineer who understands the widely taught principle that the costs of nearly all systems—say automobiles, ships, or aircraft—correlate closely and directly with their weight. This same individual will nonetheless accept without question the fact that if one attempts to take weight *out* of such a machine, its cost will dramatically *increase*! As usual, there are explanations: "The use of exotic lightweight materials *always* in-creases cost"; or, in the case of overhead, "increases in workload *always* increase costs due to the need for additional hiring, training, and facilities. . . not to mention the impact of operating with less experienced employees."

Any pragmatic manager having had the facts of life repeatedly explained by his subordinates will thus dutifully realize that the Law of Insatiable Comfort must, regrettably, be reported:

Decreased business base increases overhead. Increased business base increases overhead.

(LAW NUMBER XV)

In the words of John Newbauer of the American Institute of Aeronautics and Astronautics, "When luxuries become necessities, that's decadence!"

All Started by a Spark

Nearly all men die of their remedies,
not of their illnesses.

Moliere

Although some management aspects of the program scrutinized herein may have proved troublesome, the technical work is moving ahead spectacularly. It has been possible to add many new capabilities to the system, all so successfully that it is still months before the first test of any kind is to take place. The key to this achievement has proven to be a growing utilization of electronics, in some cases to perform functions previously undertaken only by humans. In fact, the system now only vaguely resembles the far more primitive design which surprisingly seemed so attractive back in the days when the initial proposal to undertake the project was being written. As Don Meredith once noted about another area of human endeavor, "Pro football isn't what it used to be; and it never was."

General of the Army Omar N. Bradley often quoted the old Signal Corps maxim that Congress makes a general, but only communications can make him a commander. In our zeal to emulate this truism, however, others of us have somehow managed to place ourselves in so extreme a position that it has sometimes been suggested that the side which wins the next war will be the one with the last antenna standing. As Dr. Bob Everett, President of the MITRE Corporation, has cautioned with no inconsiderable amount of concern, there are those who would have us believe:

> The American Soldier,
> His strength is as the strength of ten,
> 'Cause he has LSI.

LSI, Large Scale Integration of electronics circuitry, is indeed important. But one suspects such intangibles as courage, motivation, and initiative may still be worth more than their weight in silicon.

Nonetheless, *The Washington Star* has reported that "if past wars were won or lost in places like the playing fields of Eton, future wars will be won or lost on computer terminals." The magnitude of the

Trends in Avionics Aboard Fighter/Attack Aircraft

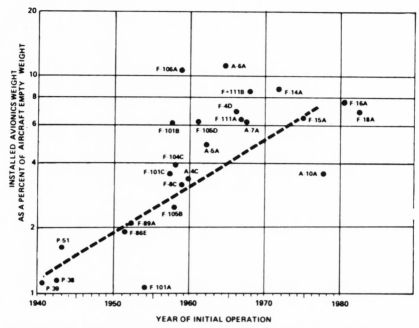

Figure 24 The fraction of many military systems which is comprised of electronics has grown rapidly for several decades, whether measured in terms of cost, weight . . . or problems.

computer explosion has been illustrated in a session at MIT where Michael Dertavzos noted that, in the next few decades, it will be feasible to store the world's knowledge in a computer for about half a billion dollars per LOC. But, in this case, an "LOC" is *not* the pedestrian "Line of Code". . . but, rather, is a "Library of Congress."

Such viewpoints do point to a trend in the proliferation of electronics which could be either productive or counterproductive, depending on how they are harnessed. The notion of computers fighting one another is *already* a reality. Much has been written about giant data processors developing codes to protect the secrecy of messages while enemy computers simultaneously seek to decipher those codes. Or, on a smaller scale, there are today computers controlling countermeasures devices in electronic warfare operations, and enemy computers managing the enemy's counter-countermeasures equipment, and friendly computers assigning counter-counter countermeasures, and. . . .

Each application of electronics seemingly leads to still another in an almost endless chain, raising the danger that electronics may indeed dominate all equipment before it can itself be controlled. Giant computers are at work designing their own offspring. . . the ultimate in electronic perpetuation. The extent of this prolific trend is examined in Figure 24, in which is presented the fraction of military fighter/interceptor/attack aircraft weight that is comprised of electronics. It has been observed that airplanes are no more than trucks in which to carry electrons around the sky. The trend with time is, unfortunately, unmistakable. Extrapolating once again, undauntedly, certain characteristics of that sole airplane which will exist a few decades from now can be derived. Namely, it will be made entirely of electronics.

As dubious as it may seem, to sustain the above well-established trend, airplanes will eventually have to be built using black boxes in place of pilots and shooting streams of electrons or photons. . . since there will be no space available for either pilots or bullets. In this space-age airplane, travel beyond the atmosphere may even be possible; but since there will be no room for conventional engines, some form of electrical propulsion will presumably be demanded to give the electron its due. Clearly the makings of science fiction. . . but the trend towards ever-increasing electronic content of aircraft does seem to deserve a skeptical reexamination before it becomes cast in silicon. Law Number XVI, the Law of Unrelenting Electrification, unabashedly predicts that:

The contribution of electronics to aviation is so great that by the year 2015 there will be no further airplane crashes. Unfortunately, there will be no further takeoffs either: avionics will then occupy 100 percent of every airplane's weight.

(LAW NUMBER XVI)

Only now, with the establishment of this Law, can it be explained what Lord Kelvin, who did so much to advance modern science, had in mind when he predicted more boldly than wisely that "aircraft flight is impossible!" All those snickers over the years can be seen to have been undeserved; he, like Calvin Coolidge, was *ahead* of his time. Law XVI would certainly indicate, however, that it was not his finest hour when he also predicted, "Radio has no future!" There can be little question that, as the Chinese proverb states, "It is difficult to prophesy, especially about the future."

The trend of filling weapon stations on modern attack aircraft with an ever-expanding array of navigation pods, radar warning pods, electronic warfare pods, self-defense missiles, target acquisition avionics pods, target illumination pods, and terrain-following radar pods brings ever-nearer the day when with impunity an aircraft will be able to take off, fly through enemy territory, accurately pinpoint its target, and return home. Unfortunately, however, there will be no store-stations left on which to carry weapons with which to attack the target. But even this may not be altogether inappropriate. With the high cost of modern air-to-ground weapons, it may prove cheaper to fly the weapons home and simply inundate the enemy with avionics pods.

A related circumstance actually occurred during World War I when the German Air Force, seeking to draw fire away from its bases, began constructing a false air strip occupied only by wooden airplanes, wooden vehicles, and wooden buildings. Unable to draw the attention of the Royal Air Force, the Germans continued to expand and improve upon the deception until finally, having spent nearly as much money as would have been required to construct a legitimate air base, they abandoned the effort in frustration. The extent of frustration was not, however, to become evident until a few days later when a single British aircraft flew down the main runway and dropped a single *wooden* bomb!

It may be that the trend toward filling all available space *within* an airplane with electronics will eventually necessitate a return to the early days of aviation when the electronics were actually trailed on a line *behind* the aircraft. According to the 1919 edition of *U.S. Army Aircraft Production Facts*, it was common practice that "airplane radio antenna for telegraph work consisted of about 300 feet of fine braided copper wire trailing below and behind the plane from a suitable reel and held in place by a lead weight of approximately 1 1/4 pounds attached to its end." (With today's emphasis on low-altitude military flying, it is doubtful that the environmental impact of such a concept would be acceptable.) Even in 1919 the practicability of such a scheme suffered some doubt in that it was duly noted, in the above book: "Mr. McCurdy, the pilot, had to pay so much attention to flying his machine that he could send only detached letters of the alphabet!"

Moving into the space age: a joint Italian/U.S. project is now underway to tow a satellite in the Earth's atmosphere from a 62 mile-long tether attached to the Space Shuttle.

In fairness, it should be noted that, as pointed out by Dr. George Heilmeier, a former Director of the Defense Advanced Research Projects Agency and currently Vice President of Texas Instruments, "If the automotive industry had progressed during the last two decades at the same rate as the semiconductor industry, a Rolls Royce would today cost only three dollars (and there would be no parking problem because automobiles would be one quarter inch on a side!)."

But, at the same time, there remain those cynics of the role of electronics in the space program who would point to instances where had a human not been on board there would have been no one available to repair the failures which were encountered in the life-support system. There are also those who might irreverently note that if it were not for the radar display screens in the cockpit, there would be no place to affix all the caution and warning stickers. The rampant use of computers is such that there are now those who refer to an airplane and its associated engines as "peripherals."

This trend is nowhere better represented than in the case of the manned bomber. The World War II B-29 contained about 10,000 electronic component parts, the B-47 approximately 20,000, the B-52 50,000 and the B-58 nearly 100,000. . . or a factor of two each generation. But this rate of growth has been eclipsed by the B-1, which is packed with microcircuits containing as many active elements on a single chip as were carried in an entire B-58. Dr. Allen Puckett, Chairman of the Board of Hughes Aircraft Company, comments—not too seriously—that "the real miracle of the Wright Brothers flight was that they accomplished it without the use of any electronics at all." He explains, "The only electrical devices in the Wright Flyer were the magneto and the spark gap in each cylinder of the engine." Today, an International L-1011 contains $4 million of avionics. . . roughly the worth of a DC-7C some twenty years earlier. In fact, about one million dollars in 1960 would have bought every microcircuit then in existence.

Not only have airplanes succumbed to the electrifying experience of embracing high technology, but so too have the missiles they shoot. The Phoenix missile, for example, contains 538,000 active circuit elements. . . contrasting markedly with its forebearer of a dozen years earlier which suffered through its existence on a mere 118 active elements. Fortunately, great strides have been made in increasing the reliability of electronic circuitry; however, correspondingly great discipline must now be exercised not to negate this gain by the un-bounded introduction of more and more circuits.

The confidence the creators of such marvels of electronic wizardry hold in their progeny might be gleaned from a recent issue of *Lockheed Life*, an internal company paper. It is therein dutifully reported that Lockheed employs a squadron of carrier pigeons to carry messages between its Sunnyvale plant and its Santa Cruz test site in California.

James McNeill Whistler, the renowned American artist, seemed to have had a personalized premonition of just how different our world would be had it not been for advancements in microelectronics. Late in his career, he looked back upon a less than successful experience as a cadet at West Point during which he is said to have failed a course in chemistry: "If silicon had been a gas," he lamented, "I might have been a major general."

Even in the presence of this great promise of onrushing technology, one wonders if something might have been overlooked. One wonders if somewhere deep in the recesses of the computers in the Library of Congress there might not still be that passage from the now-aging book on Medal of Honor recipients which decribes the deeds of one such honored individual. It tells of a soldier who single-handedly saved his unit from the withering fire of an enemy machine gun; how he first ran forward and finally, after being wounded repeatedly, crawled forward to destroy the threatening weapon with a hand grenade. The author of the book describing the action, unable to contain his skepticism of science any longer, concluded his narrative with the words: "It was another great victory for American technology."

Bit by Bit

It is at this point that the program which is the subject of this tale unexpectedly encounters one of the most ethereal, obtrusive, and recalcitrant substances to challenge technical managers since it was first discovered that the universe consists of earth, fire, water, and software. . .the latter a substance which seemingly creeps into systems to an ever-increasing extent. . . even in instances wherein its very need may be in doubt. It is somewhat as Mark Twain has noted, "Banks will lend you money, if you can prove you don't need it."

Considerable strain can be seen to be building within the acquisition process as engineers and managers seek to produce useful products while complying with the plethora of laws that have come into existence, both natural and man-made. Indeed, laws, like regulations, seem to grow like weeds. Complicating the effort to comply with all the regulations is the often contradictory guidance given by official bodies, such as the various committees of Congress. In fact, in several recent instances the Congress has gone so far as to *legislate* the initial deployment dates for new systems as part of the Appropriations Act. In doing so the dates are *law*. It is not yet clear what the exact liability may be for managers of those programs should they fail to meet the prescribed dates, especially in instances where the Congress subsequently cuts their budgets, but it *is* clear that this has not significantly reduced the stress within the acquisition process.

The dilemma faced by those involved in the acquisition process can be typified by the difficulty of complying with both Law Number IX and Law XVI, simultaneously. The first of these laws ordains that the cost of hardware (e.g., airplanes) increases *rapidly* with time. To comply with this stringent requirement in the time period when there will be no additional space or weight left in an airplane (since the entire volume will, according to Law XVI, already be filled with electronics) places *severe* demands on a designer. Optimally, what is needed is something that can be added to airplanes and other systems which weighs *nothing*, yet is *very* costly, and violates none of the physical

100

Trends in Software Growth

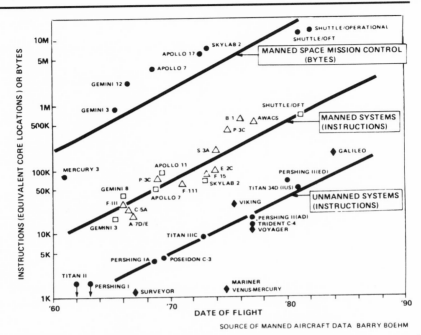

Figure 25   Software, almost nonexistent a few decades ago, is rapidly becoming the dominant element in the design of most major systems.

laws of the universe, such as the law of gravitation or the laws of thermodynamics.

This might appear to be an insurmountable challenge. However, as a result of the traditional ingenuity characteristic of system designers it can be reported with confidence that such an ingredient has already been found.

It is called. . . *software.*

A principal property of software, the phantom of modern technology (a "riddle wrapped in a mystery inside an enigma," to use Churchill's words), can be seen in Figure 25, which illustrates the trend toward ever-increasing quantities of software in any given family of systems.*

There are in fact three separate growth modes evidenced by software. The first two of these are from generation-to-generation of new

---

*The groupings of the data shown in Figure 25 into the categories of unmanned and manned systems is interesting, but is most likely a figment of the rather modest data base available with which to treat this topic. . .although there can be little doubt of the reality of the growth trend within a given class.

items of equipment (from an F-4 aircraft to an F-14) and from version-to-version of a given item of equipment (Titan I to Titan II to Titan III), respectively. The third growth mode, an internal growth mode, reflects the increase in quantity of software from the time the magnitude of a given job is initially scoped until it has actually been completed. This is often the most exasperating mode of software growth. It has been accurately stated that if you automate a mess, you get an automated mess. Figure 25 addresses the former two modes and suggests a growth rate on the order of a factor of ten every ten years.*

Law Number XVII, the Law of the Piranha, has its origin in the fact that many contractors are devotees of the "Big Bang" Theory of Software Development:

Software is like entropy. It is difficult to grasp, weighs nothing, and obeys the Second Law of Thermodynamics; i.e., it always increases.

(LAW NUMBER XVII)

As the old addage states, once you open a can of worms the only way to get them back inside is to use a bigger can.

Large-scale use of software can probably be traced back to the SAGE (Semi-Automatic Ground Environment) air defense system of the late 1950's which was implemented using computers comprised of 58,000 vacuum tubes and consuming 1.5 megawatts of power. The real-time operating program for this computer contained about 100,000 instructions (backed by support programs of 112 *million* instructions). A subsequent ballistic missile defense system, Safeguard, contained 2.2 million instructions of which 735 thousand were real time. There are those who would suggest that the contribution of such degrees of complexity will be excelled only by the projected advent of the WOM, the write-only memory.

Various studies have been conducted which suggest that over the last 25 years the hardware/software portions of the cost of major systems are shifting from an initial 80/20 hardware/software ratio to a ratio approaching 20/80 in the decade ahead. It can be safely reported that the problems encountered in development programs have managed to stay abreast of this trend. Further, it has been reported that the net effect of the computer revolution may turn out to

---

* The author is indebted to Stephen L. Copps for his assistance in collecting the data presented in Figure 25.

be no more than that we can create our errors more efficiently.

The Department of Defense estimates that in 1980 it spent $3 billion for embedded software (presumably a reference to software at rest) and in 1990 will expend $30 billion. It also points out that in 1980 there were 240,000 programmers in the U.S. The choice for the rest of us thus seems clear: either learn to manage software tasks more efficiently or start learning to program! Software is, in the vernicular, eating our lunch. . . a byte at a time.

Actually, software exhibits many of the same properties as hardware. It is subject to human error (typically one error per 100 source lines of code), "reliability" problems, and high penalties for failure to discover problems early in development effort. Dr. Barry Boehm of TRW has collected data which show the cost of correcting software errors at various points in a development activity relative to the cost incurred if the error is discovered in the coding phase. The cost is a factor of five greater when not discovered until the acceptance test phase and a factor of fifteen greater when uncovered in the operational phase. It is left to Weinberg's Second Law to observe that if builders built buildings the way programmers wrote programs, then the first woodpecker that came along would destroy civilization!

A classic example of the perversity of software was encountered in the Mariner program when on the Mariner 1 flight the lack of a single dash over a symbol in a little-used routine (the guidance module for failed doppler radar) resulted in a multimillion dollar spacecraft striking out on its own to explore the distant universe instead of observing Venus as its human masters had intended. But if software is perverse it is not without some redeeming virtues. The next Mariner flight was saved when the same set of equations (with the dash safely in place) managed to keep Mariner 2 on target in spite of an uncontrollable roll in the launch vehicle which caused loss of ground contact 75 times before full lock was reestablished.

In a Department of Defense report on software note is made of the fact that some problems do remain in the area of software management. . . and then a list of 86 examples is presented!

But if the state-of-the-art in managing software development is in some respects primitive, the acronymical language used to cloud the art from those managers necessarily thrust onto the periphery of such activity has reached a high degree of maturity indeed. This language is laced with a veritable core-dump of bauds, bits and bytes, MIPS, MOPS and BOPS. In fact, the highest order of acronymical language thus far in use appears to have been created by the software specialists working on command and control systems. . . thus effectively thwarting all those senior executives who may have had the audacity to think it was *their* role to command, or perhaps *even* to control. But the unquestioned greatest semantical contribution of the software art is the term originally coined to describe one-million floating point operations but which can be seen herein to have much broader applicability in describing entire programs or even entire groups of programs—i.e., the "megaflop."

Off Again, Off Again

What's the use? Yesterday an egg,
tomorrow a feather duster.
Mark Fenderson, ca. 1900

Incessant changes in objectives, funding, and boundary conditions begin to plague our project under the guise of either reacting to budgetary pressures or "leapfrogging forward." This does, of course, prompt the question of whether we might more often than not be better off to just keep that first frog. As the Chinese proverb notes, "If change is not necessary, it is necessary not to change." Bert Lance put it even more succinctly: "If it ain't broke," he said, "don't fix it." But, alas, the prevailing view rejects the above wisdom in favor of Heraclitus' perspective, "Nothing endures but change."

The common belief that major programs can be turned on and off as water faucets while they move through their various phases has resulted in senior government and industry managers spending more time seeking to keep projects alive than in seeing to their proper execution. In fact, it sometimes appears that program participants and fund-providers may have rather different things in mind when they embrace the seemingly mutual objective of overseeing a project's execution.

The image of managers striving to accomplish difficult and challenging tasks, only to see funds reduced and goals changed at each step along the way, sadly reminds one of a peripatetic Charlie Brown repeatedly seeking to kick a football only to have some Lucy snatch it away at each critical moment. The only apparent advantage to having the world changing so fast is that it's not possible to be wrong *all* the time.

The roller-coaster lifestyle of many a program is exemplified by the experience of the Air Force's Satellite Communication System, AFSATCOM. Figure 26 traces the funding level for the program as it ricocheted through the Congress. During the year examined — just *one* year out of many in the program's lifetime — the program manager was faced with a projected budget swing ranging from $72M to $19M. . .and never knew the correct figure until *three* months *into* the year. Furthermore, these data do not even reflect the puts and

Turbulence in the Acquisition Process
Example: AFSATCOM

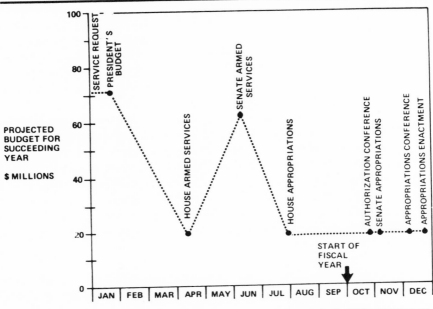

SOURCE: FY 80 APPROPRIATIONS DATA

Figure 26 Sudden changes in a program's projected funding can be extremely disruptive, expensive, and demotivating. Unfortunately, such changes are commonplace. The data shown reflect only those potential changes occurring during the final phase of the funding process; similar turbulence is often experienced over the preceding several years.

takes which occurred in the process leading to obtaining the President's approval prior to congressional action ever being initiated. One might believe that approval by the President of the United States and by the Secretary of the Whole Defense might have some meaning; but alas, that was not the case. It thus becomes apparent why most contractors have routinely added vice-presidents of marketing; why many are now installing vice-presidents of congressional relations, and a few are actively recruiting vice-presidents of clairvoyance. (One major industrial firm actually released a press notice informing the world that it was appointing a new "Vice Prescient.") But it must be stated in defense of the present process that there is one residual advantage: if you don't know where you are going, any road, according to the Turkish proverb, will get you there.

It is not contractors alone who are confused by this process. Answering a question as to whether a new thrust in basic research introduced with not inconsiderable fanfare into the FY84 budget would be continued into 1985, a Senior Policy Analyst assigned to the White House indicated that he could not possibly make such a projection, stating, "In this environment, '85 is like infinity."

A related situation was faced by the Army's Ballistic Missile Defense program, which wandered over halfway through one fiscal year with one house of Congress cutting the President's proposed budget *for that year* in half and the other leaving it unscathed. The dilemma faced by management in such perilous cases is that to make a decision to reduce the spending rate in order to protect against the eventuality that the lower figure might prevail makes the lower budget essentially a *fait accompli*; that is, the funds truly will *not* be needed. But if, on the other hand, the spending rate is *not* reduced and the lower figure *does* subsequently become reality when the issue is finally settled well over half way through the fiscal year, the program manager falls in violation of the anti-deficiency law.

The choice is thus, on the one hand, to undermine one's position or, on the other, to engage in a game of fiscal chicken. As the saying goes, it is the kind of decision that could affect you the rest of your life . . .if you lived that long.

The Precision Location and Strike System, PLSS, has endured a similarly harrowing existence. In one recent year the House Armed Services Committee added money to the funding requested by the President, and the Senate Armed Services Committee zeroed the budget. The following year, the Senate Armed Services Committee doubled the funding request and the House recommended zero. Thus is derived the expression, "a firm maybe."

This process reached its penultimate in the 97th Congress, late one Monday morning, when the U.S. Senate, as described by *Newsweek*, "in effect, voted to decide whether to vote to decide whether to reconsider a decision not to vote." In the words of a Colorado State Senator, "There's something in here to offend everybody."

During the Senate debate on the FY84 budget for the much-suffering MX missile program over 500 amendments were offered for consideration. This is known as the "Ready. . .Fire. . .Aim" school of management.

An even more innovative process has recently been gaining widespread acceptance in budgeting circles: that of cutting budgets for the development of a piece of hardware as a punishment for having encountered technical problems. As implausible as this may seem, examples abound. . . such as *Aerospace Daily's* routine report of one congressional action affecting the GSRS program: "The committee cut the $30 million request in half because it felt the Army was taking too long to develop the system." This seems to fit the category of one of those fundamentally poor ideas that never worked out.

In the case of the long-tormented LANTIRN program, the FY83 Authorization Act stated: "The Secretary of the Air Force may not enter into any contract for the production of the. . .system until after a competitive demonstration between the LANTIRN system and the suitably modified version of the Navy's F/A-18 aircraft FLIR system has been carried out."

Straightforward enough. Except that the Senate Appropriations Act for the same year contained the following guidance: "None of the funds made available by this act shall be used for any competition between the currently approved LANTIRN system and any other system. . . ."

In the words of the Ambassador to the Court of Saint James; "Compromise makes a good umbrella, but a poor roof. . . ."

That the phenomenon of "involvement" is on the upswing is suggested by the following data, which examine the fraction of major* programs suffering budget changes by congressional action in recent years:

Year	Percent of Programs Having Budget Changed by Congress (Relative to President's Request)
1977	28
1978	42
1979	47
1980	55
1981	63

Seeking to manage literally hundreds of research and development projects from the lofty heights of the U. S. Congress is like trying to herd chickens on horseback.

Although including procurement as well as research and development, the numbers in the above totals exclude the large number of instances where direction was given via legislative *language* as opposed to *fiscal* action. . .and, by and large, apply to a period

---

*"Major" Programs as considered here are those included in the System Acquisition Report Submitted to Congress.

when the same political party controlled the White House and both Houses of Congress! So-called "language" stipulations can be every bit as troublesome as budget "adjustments" (read "cuts"). In 1975, for example, one House directed that no funds be spent on *fixed* ICBM's. Both did agree, however, that funds should be spent. Happily, the conference committee resolved the impasse, but not until the project's planning had been placed in a quandary.

Similarly, in the case of the Continuous Airborne Patrol version of the MX Missile system, the authorization report one year prohibited any work on this concept while the appropriation report limited this (*non*) work to ten-million dollars!

Although the most readily available data happen to relate to actions of the Congress, that institution is by no means the only cause of turbulence. . . just the easiest to track because of its not inconsiderable propensity to generate documentation. Its actions are, however, particularly profound because they generally occur *after* the start of the year in which funds are to be expended (Law Number XIX). For example, the then newly negotiated Advanced Attack Helicopter program once saw its funding halved by the Administration, resulting in a series of contract renegotiations which were completed just in time to see the Congress double the program's budget and set off the third round of contract negotiations the same year. A report attributed to a Spanish Civil War communique pretty well sums up the situation: "Our troops advanced today without losing a meter of ground."

The degree of micromanagement which is extant is evidenced by one Congressional action on the Trident budget request. After a scathing assessment, the committee proceeded to cut the budget by 0.0009 percent! The principal beneficiaries of fiscal instability are those who would seek to eliminate all vestiges of accountability for a program's progress or who would like to discourage long-term investment in a program by the contractor. Further, such impact is not limited to the prime contractor, but instead cascades through an entire network of subcontractors and sometimes thousands of vendors like a string of falling dominos. In a typical year a large firm will have well over 10,000 contracts with other firms. The B-1B program alone has 5,200 subcontractors and suppliers. What does seem to be an indisputable truth is that no corporation could survive were its board of directors to become as intimately involved in operations as does the 535-member board which oversees the acquisition process.

And the above omits altogether the omnipresent changes in the overall business climate to which contractors must adjust. One example is the prime rate which determines the cost of their borrowings; a rate which changed once every six months in the

1960's, once a month in the 1970's, and once a *week* early in the 1980's.

The law which relates to the above-mentioned lack of program stability is known as the Law of Universal Agitation and is derived from studies of Brownian movement among programs:

> **There are only three kinds of programs which suffer incessant budget tampering: those which are behind schedule, those which are on schedule, and those which used to be ahead of schedule.**
>
> **(LAW NUMBER XVIII)**

The source of these changes often originates at the highest levels in government, sometimes beginning with the President and working upward through the congressional staffs.

The solution to this dynamicism has been discovered by none other than the Boy Scouts of America in one of their continuous succession of questionnaires to members asking what the young men would like to see changed. Among the more common answers: "Stop making changes."

Work and the Theory of Relativity

Know the right timing.
Diogenes Laertius

Although a number of problems are emerging in our perhaps-not-so-imaginary program, when one considers the extenuating circumstances it can generally be concluded that these are actually not too severe. The most annoying problem of all has been the continual nuisance of schedule slippages on items which somehow always find their way onto the critical path. Fortunately, there is a law which points the way to a resolution of such difficulties. It is inspired by the practice used in the U.S. Congress of stopping the wall clocks in the chamber when a new fiscal year is about to start if the enabling spending legislation has not yet been passed.

Sir William S. Gilbert, standing on a train station platform overlooking an empty track, observed, "Saturday afternoons, although coming at regular and well-foreseen intervals, always take this railway by surprise."

In competitive, time-sensitive markets, managers are simultaneously challenged on three fronts. Not only must they produce a desirable product at a reasonable price, but, in addition, they must deliver their output to the marketplace in a timely manner. This urgency is characteristic of a large variety of products, irrespective of whether the aforementioned pressure arises from perishability of the product, the need to rapidly exploit some technological breakthrough, or merely to keep up with demand.

However, in environments wherein only one source of an item is available, an altogether different set of dynamics prevails. Consider, as but one example, the problem faced by the U.S. Congress as each year, in addition to a myriad of other crucial tasks, it pursues the matter of approving a budget for each of the federal departments. For one reason or another, the Congress has apparently found it increasingly difficult to complete this task prior to the beginning of the year in which the money is to be spent. There have even been attempts to organize task forces to deal head-on with the problem of legislative procrastination, but thus far it has been impossible to agree on whether such efforts might not themselves be deferred.

111

112

Increasing Length of Budget Approval Process

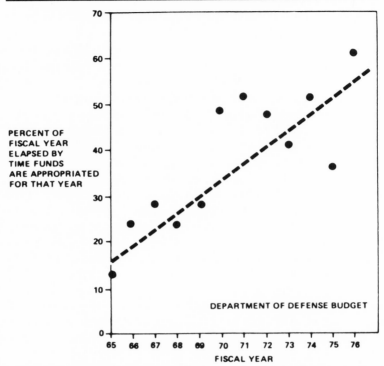

Figure 27   The process of preparing a budget and obtaining its approval used to consume an increasing period of time each year until a drastic step was taken at the end of Fiscal Year 1976. . . after which the process continued to consume an increasing period of time each year.

The data in Figure 27 display how in each fiscal year the date at which funds are finally appropriated has tended to slide further and further into the year. This problem recently culminated, in the case of the defense budget, in a circumstance wherein the appropriation act did not become law until the year was more than half over! The challenge posed to those charged with executing that budget can be imagined. . .particularly those unfortunate managers whose requested budget was halved midway through the year!

What the future portended for those same managers could be glimpsed by projecting forward in time the trend line in Figure 27. The inevitable conclusion seemed to be that it would be only about a decade until the situation reached crisis proportions; i.e., the budget would not be approved until the year was altogether past. As Perkins McGuire would say, "With the past coming down the road so fast, we are going to have to address it in the future."

Fully recognizing this dilemma, the Congress proceeded to rectify the intensifying problem with both alacrity and decisiveness. Less imaginative managers in private industry, given the same circumstances, might have resorted to such conventional techniques as eliminating some of the 18 votes taken each year on large segments of the budget (an outgrowth of the old "vote early and vote often" school of politics), or even to a process of expediting the budget cycle by combining various steps in the review process, or perhaps even by resorting to multiyear funding or multiyear budgeting.

As luck would have it, however, no such pedestrian approaches were needed. They would have demanded an uncommon amount of common sense. The obvious solution, and that seized upon by the Congress, was, of course, to pass a law changing the definition of the fiscal year, thereafter slipping it neatly into compliance with the time it was actually taking to complete the task of preparing a budget. All of which simply proves once again the old saw: Things may be desperate, but they aren't yet serious.

(The Congress actually may not have orginated this process but instead may merely have emulated the practice of the U.S. Naval Observatory of occasionally adding a second to a day to keep clocks in synchronization with the Earth's movement. Such a "leap-second" was added on the last day of January in 1983 and was reported by the Associated Press as "stopping the clocks to allow the Earth to catch up.")

This is not to suggest that the newly established Congressional budgeting trend is not itself disconcerting. In the years immediately succeeding the above harmonization of the calendar, budgets were approved 0, 4, 22 and 21 percent, respectively, of the way through the *new* year.

In the case of fiscal year 1983 the process fell so far behind that, faced with the arrival of the *1984* budget request before the FY83 budget had been acted upon, the lame-duck 97th Congress *never did* produce a FY83 Defense appropriations act. Rather, the Defense Department proceeded under a year-long series of continuing resolutions.

Hence, although budgets are still being approved after the fiscal year is well underway, they nonetheless have generally turned out to be the earliest they have ever been late.

The *Orlando Sentinel* found the sports-world analogy to the above practice when it reported that a Florida State offensive guard—"a muscular 5'11" 240-pounder with powerful legs — recorded the fastest time in his weight division in the 12-minute run."

The methodology pioneered by the Congress, it should be mentioned, has now been adopted by industry. One firm, which had widely advertised amid much fanfare that the first flight of a new commercial jet aircraft would take place "before the end of the year," later announced that the goal had indeed been met — the successful flight "took place on the 32nd of December."

The essential element that made this resolution of a nasty problem possible was, of course, the fact that there is only one Congress available, and if this one does not produce a budget by any given time, there is no danger of another competitive Congress stepping in and producing one of its own. It can be safely inferred that such latitude for problem solving is by no means restricted to governmental bodies, but is attendant to any entity functioning in a sole-source environment. There is nothing profound in such an observation; it is only one more manifestation of the Golden Rule: He who has the gold, makes the rules.

Professor C. Northcote Parkinson, in the well-known law which bears his name, examined the effort devoted to activities which are time-constrained. Law Number XIX of the present monograph is a reciprocal to Parkinson's proposition and considers the case wherein the *work* to be performed is constrained. Parkinson's Law pointed out, in essence, that work expands to fit the time prescribed. In contradistinction, the Law of Inconstancy of Time points out:

In a noncompetitive process, time expands to fit the work prescribed.

(LAW NUMBER XIX)

Striving To Be Average

Cave canem.[*]

Latin Proverb

There is a law which confirms the suspicion (held by a majority of people) that very few people come up to the average. This is in fact beginning to be widely suspected among the participants in our somewhat beleagured program. This is particularly true now that more and more people are having to be added to the project to offset the added work caused by the schedule slips which somehow continue to occur in spite of the enlightened management techniques being employed.

Robert Frost was among the first to note that the world is full of willing people: "some willing to work," he pointed out, and "the rest willing to let them."

The contribution made by a group of people working in a common endeavor tends to be highly concentrated in the achievements of a few members of that group. The degree of this concentration is observed to obey a fundamental law, as indicated by the data in Figure 28. It is seen that the great predominance of output is produced by a disproportionately small segment of the participants, with the same law seeming to apply whether one is addressing authors, pilots, engineers, policemen, or football players. As one "digs deeper into the barrel," to increase the manpower assigned to a given task, the average output is merely driven downward and, ultimately, large numbers of participants are added with hardly any increase in productivity at all (unless, of course, changes in work methods are also introduced). Conversely, substantial reductions in manning —eliminating the least productive contributors—can be made with little impact on overall output. In fact, the least productive half of all participants seems to generate *no more* than 20 percent of the total output. Bob Whalen, general manager of Global Analytics, Inc., refers to programs drawing upon this latter half as "Statue of Liberty Programs"..."Give me your tired, your poor, your huddled masses...!"

It might be more accurate to describe the above observation as merely a generalization or corollary of V. Pareto's work published in

---

[*]"Beware of the dog."

Concentration of Productivity

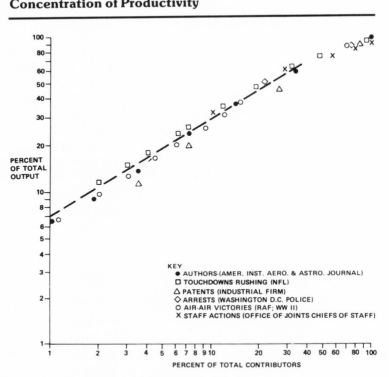

Figure 28   In virtually any undertaking it is found that a very small fraction of the participants produces a very large fraction of the accomplishments. It must, in fairness, be pointed out that a very small fraction of the participants also produces a very large fraction of the problems.

1897, in which it is demonstrated that the proportion of people with an income N is proportionate to $1/N^{1.5}$. In words, there are those who make things happen; there are those who watch things happen; and there are those who ask what happened.

The results presented in Figure 28 are probably understated, since the data base considers only participants who made at least some contribution, such as obtaining one patent, when in reality there are many who obtained no patents. Further, there are unquestionably those who produce negative output, such as the worker who makes so many mistakes that a great deal of the time of other potentially productive workers is consumed in rectifying the problems the former has created. Only about one-third of the workers typically achieve a level of contribution equal to the average of all those who contribute. In a moment of frustration a second-string National Football League quarterback summed up the problem: "It's hard to soar like an eagle if you are surrounded by turkeys!"

All of which leads to the productivity law, more rigorously known as the Second Law of Averages, which relates to the allocation of manpower. It can be stated as follows:

One-tenth of the participants produce at least one-third of the output, and increasing the number of participants merely reduces the average output.

(LAW NUMBER XX)

Amazingly, the top 1 percent produce nearly 50 times the per capita output of the bottom half.

As has often been pointed out, when an individual item can be produced only at a financial loss, it is very, very difficult to make it up on volume. Or, as the railroad porter explained to a passenger who challenged the porter's suggestion that his average tip ran about ten dollars, "Of course, very few people come up to the average."

The Amoeba Instinct

The meek shall inherit the earth. . .
But the strong shall retain the mineral rights.
Graffito at a U.S. University

For some months things have been looking dismal but now they are becoming serious. It is evident that if some incisive management action is not taken the program could find itself in not inconsiderable difficulty. Fortunately, the appropriate step is widely recognized among the managers at all levels. In fact, it is the subject of a law of its own: Reorganization.

A Secretary of Defense once signaled the demise of an elaborate reorganization being enthusiastically endorsed by the author of these laws, said endorsement being marked by a profusion of the classical organization charts showing all the requisite little squares and branches, with the four-word eulogy, "New tree. . . same monkeys."

The problem with reorganizing was perhaps best summarized some 2000 years ago in the following remarks attributed to Petronius Arbiter:

We trained hard . . . but it seemed that every time we were beginning to form up into a team, we would be reorganized. I was to learn later in life that we tend to meet any new situation by reorganizing. And a wonderful method it can be of creating the illusion of progress while producing confusion, inefficiency and demoralization.

The popularity of reorganization might best be viewed from the perspective espoused in the advertisement placed in the *Wall Street Journal* by the United Technologies Corporation which dutifully notes: "When forty million people believe in a dumb idea, it's still a dumb idea."

Even the term "reorganize" is a semantic nonsequitur. To "reorganize" implies that one must have been organized. If one were organized, why then would one want to reorganize?

Playing with blocks seems to be inherent in man. In fact, the proclivity to play with blocks seems to be on the increase. One can draw this conclusion from studies of organizations at all levels. In

The Urge to Purge

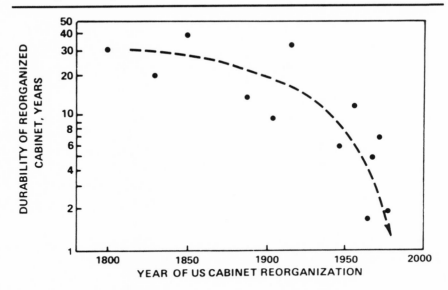

Figure 29 The tendency to reorganize with ever-increasing frequency is a phenomenon observed in organizations ranging from the most modest enterprises to the Cabinet of the United States.

seeking a centerpiece of evidence one may as well begin at the very top: the U.S. Cabinet. Figure 29 thus examines the frequency of reorganization of the Cabinet throughout the history of the nation. The observed trend is one of an ever-increasing pace of reorganization. . . moving inexorably toward a condition wherein the time-durability of any given organizational state will soon become negative. The meaning of this is that it may actually become necessary to organize *before* reorganizing. That such a state should come to exist is a sad testimonial to the great American tradition that if one reorganizes with sufficient frequency, it is possible to altogether avoid ever becoming organized. It has been said that this is a fundamental factor in the U.S.'s historic record of dominance on the international scene. Generally, in the midst of critical events we become confused. But this, in turn, often causes our adversaries to become confused. But *we* are *used* to being confused, and thus. . .

Bodies of all types, including government, industry and universities, have on occasion organized committees to study one principal form of confusion called reorganization. One high-level committee examining possible reorganization of parts of the Federal Government met its premature demise because the committee itself had to be reorganized. Another job which met a similar fate in a reorganization was that of the Executive Associate Director for Reorganization and Management in the Office of Management and Budget. . . the ill-fated czar of governmental turf rights.

It is possible to visualize many graphic organization charts apropos to various organizations. For the less stable dictatorships in the world, an organization chart with various blocks crossed out in advance with a large "X" has been suggested. The United Nations would be represented with a set of boxes joined together in a circle; the U.S. Congress with a single horizontal chain of 535 separate boxes. In the case of U.S. industrial practice, it has been suggested that the system can be represented by the classical organization chart but with little stringers going to and fro from the bottom boxes directly into the top box. As noted some years ago by one Mr. Al Capone, to the dismay of those occupying the intermediate boxes, "You can get more with a kind word and a gun than you can get with a kind word."

Just as military commanders have known for years that battles are always fought on the edge of the map in use, contract disputes are always fought on the interfaces of responsibility of the respective participants.

The purpose of many reorganizations has been said to be to separate the "men from the boys." However, the failing comes in the lack of recognition that the idea is to keep the "*men*." When a block is *retained* on the newly reorganized organization chart, it is generally lauded as being indispensable. But all is not lost; when a block is *deleted* from the new chart, it is duly announced that it was simply irreplaceable. *All* are thus winners. Clarence Darrow remarked "When I was a boy, I was told anybody could become president; I'm beginning to believe it." The net result, however, is that we may be reorganizing ourselves right out of existence. Many modern managers, it is suspected, would find irresistible the tendency to run around rearranging the ashtrays on the deck of the Titanic in the ship's final hours.

In summary, to paraphrase a comment by Dr. Clark Kerr about another type of entity, organizations are collections of loosely knit individuals bound together by a mutual fear of reorganization. The bottom line, then, is recorded in the Law of the Nest, which is itself simply a restatement of Martin Luther's observation that "it makes a difference whose ox is gored." The Law notes:

It is better to be the reorganizer than the reorganizee.

(LAW NUMBER XXI)

Nowhere has this been more openly recognized than on the organization chart of the IBM's corporate office. . .wherein one finds none other than a "Vice-President for Reorganization."*

"The race is not always to the swift or the battle to the strong." But, as Damon Runyon tells us, "That is the way to bet."

---

*The author assumes that the existence of this office has been unaffected by reorganizations taking place since it was last seen in November 1981.

Hail on the Chief

There go the people. I am their leader.
I must follow them.
A Former Mayor of Boston

The problems plaguing the program are proving to be more
intractable than should be expected when such clever
management techniques are in use. A widening gulf is in
fact growing between top managment and the rest of the
work force, exacerbated by the amount of time being
consumed in the negotiations to sell the entire product line
to the company's principal competitor. Clearly a further
decisive step is needed to improve both the morale and the
quality of working level paticipants. Having abandoned a
suggestion to cancel all vacations unless morale improves,
attention turns to the latter of the abovementioned
problems and three substantive techniques for its resolution
are found and promptly implemented. One is to provide a
more exalted title for each of the current managers.
Another is to hire a consultant. The third is for the com-
pany's top executive to personally assume command of the
project.

Law Number XXII addresses the natural superiority of more exalted
officials in achieving results; somewhat as George Kaufman may have
had in mind when he wrote, "Two men were killed in the construction
work in Panama. One was English, the other a laborer."

It is widely recognized in management circles that by assigning
people of high rank to manage a task, the chance of problems occurring with that task will be minimized. This is somewhat analogous
to the author's corollary to the Peter Principle: "*Decisions* rise to the
management level where the person making them is least qualified to
do so." As various experts, each involved in narrow segments of an
issue, find themselves unable to reach agreement, the matter is
elevated for adjudication to a senior manager who has no particular
expertise or currency in *any* of the factors under contention. This
concept is frequently put to practice when a program suffering some
discomfiture is handed from, say, a director to a vice president in
order to "straighten things out." But, as Lieutenant General Dick

Henry explains it, "Many companies are *very* loyal to their senior employees. Some even independent of talent."

The viewpoint of executives who usurp the function of lesser managers only to discover no improvement results from the change has been well expressed by a baseball manager who yanked his center-fielder after he dropped three straight fly balls. Having decided to *personally* take the place of the errant fielder, the manager suffered the ignominy of himself dropping what proved to be the game-winning pop fly. Returning to the dugout and the penetrating stares of his players, the dismayed manager explained, pointing at his predecessor, "He had that position so fouled up that now *no one* can play it."

The payoff from this escalatory approach in industry is, however, difficult to measure because the necessary data are once again mercifully unavailable. A rather good measure is, however, possible for government program managers. This latter measure is very likely applicable to industry managers as well, based on the theorem of Equal Escalation in Rank, whereby companion pairs of industry/government managers working on the same project must be of equal elevation in order to satisfy the respective rules of engagement and protocol.

Specifically, the theory of superior performance by organizational superiors would demand that were a plot made of some measure of the occurrence of problems in a program against the rank of the manager involved, a steeply decreasing trend in problems would be observed as rank increases. Such a plot is presented in Figure 30 — except, that is, for the steeply decreasing trend.

The results seem to verify the addage attributed by some to the industrial world: "Rank times IQ is a constant."

The contemptuous behavior of hardware for the exalted, which is reflected in the figure, has undoubtedly already been suspected by any practitioner of these unnatural laws; it will therefore be no surprise to learn that hardware has equal disdain for managers of *all* ranks. In the case of hardware management, it can thus be reliably stated that the superior is frequently inferior. Coach Tommy Prothro described the situation accurately: "Our team is well balanced. We have problems everywhere."

The parameter examined in this assessment, wherein each data point in the figure represents a particular program, is the parameter which has been afforded the most widespread attention in criticism of program management, namely, the ability (inability) to control cost. Cost problems are found to be woefully disrespectful of rank.

Cost Growth During Program Manager's Tenure

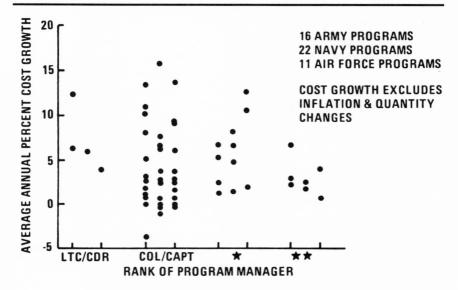

SOURCE: DOD SELECTED ACQUISITION REPORTS (COST DATA)

Figure 30   Program managers within the Department of Defense generally hold rank spanning from Lieutenant Colonel/   Commander to two-star Flag Officer, depending on such factors as the size and importance of the program they direct. Unfortunately, cost growth shows little respect for rank.

Somehow programs and their attendant hardware are inexplicably not as impressed by who you are as by what you do.

Worse yet, a study reported in *The Economist* concerning the introduction of new products into the *commercial* marketplace found that 58 percent of all innovations ultimately fail; except, that is, for those originated by top management. . . which fail at a rate of 74 percent.

This insensitivity of the occurrence of problems to the titular grandeur of the immediate management would seem to suggest that Socrates and his faithful student companion, Plato, did not go far enough when they concluded, perhaps not altogether surprisingly, that *philosophers* should be kings. Apparently it should have been added that program managers should be *privates*. . . for no other reason than privates cost less than generals (and vice-presidents) and seem to perform at least as well. It is noteworthy that this conclusion has apparently already been partially reached by the Air Force, which only recently appointed its first noncommissioned officer program manager. The track record to be established by this individual is eagerly awaited in all quarters. For a variety of reasons.

But perhaps the most important lesson to be learned from the Greek philosophers by those who would be progenitors of laws such as these was succinctly captured in more recent times by a young girl, obviously enamored with the virtues of brevity, as she wrote an essay on the life of Socrates: "Socrates was a philosopher," she wrote. "He went around pointing out errors in the way things were done," she continued. "They fed him hemlock," she concluded.

Nonetheless, returning to the problem of senior managers being denied their due respect at the hands of complex undertakings, the argument will, of course, be made by higher-ranking officials that higher-ranking officials have more difficult programs to manage. But it can be equally argued that those same individuals command more authority and enjoy access to more resources with which to avoid problems. . . and that the allocation of program management assignments is made by none other than high-ranking officials themselves and, as such, complaints of this type might be suspect!

The Law of Equipartition of Misfortune (sometimes referred to as the Law of Rank Insubordination) is thus derived:

Rank does not intimidate hardware. Neither does the lack of rank.

(LAW NUMBER XXII)

It has already been noted that no less a body than the United States Congress has recently taken to *legislating* the dates by which certain equipment development programs are to be completed. The failure by the Congress to recognize the above law would suggest that this august body is laying the groundwork for a profound lesson in humility. Meg Greenfield, writing about the challenge of policymaking in Washington, accurately observes, "The ordeal, the setting for failure, is the effort to make any of it happen."

The irreverence of hardware for officialdom has long been recognized by individuals working at test ranges. Among these enthusiasts it is an article of faith that the incidence of flight test failures is directly proportional to the square of the size of the crowd multiplied by the rank of the senior observing official. Although widely held, this explanation does not exactly match the experimental evidence. . . which displays even *greater* perversity. The interpretation may possibly be found in Lt. Gen. Glenn Kent's observation that in counting rank we should not merely refer to a Rear Admiral or Major General as "two-stars," but rather should adopt the European system for counting points on antlers of game animals. Using this technique, the points on *both* sides are counted; and a Major General thus becomes not a two- but a *four*-star force. . . thereby accurately matching the empirial evidence for test failures.

Examples of this general phenomenon are rampant throughout history. There was, for example, the great sailing ship, Vassa, newly launched into the harbor of Stockholm in the witness of an enormous gathering of royalty. . . only to float tentatively a few hundred yards, overturn in full view of all present, and ignominiously become a sunk cost. This demonstrated conclusively that the metacenter of a ship desires to be located in a certain relationship to the center of gravity irrespective of the amount of royalty, cannon fire, and band music brought to bear.

It was just such a phenomenon that led to the abort, on worldwide television, of the first attempt to launch the Space Shuttle. In this instance, a set of computers which had been tested repeatedly turned out to have inherent in them a hidden malfunction mode which would preclude synchronization with the backup computer. The chances of the timing clock falling into this mode were about 1 in 100. When, then, was this malfunction finally encountered in actual operation? Why, on the very first launch attempt, of course. That this could be explained on a statistical basis challenges plausibility. The explanation necessarily resides in the above discussion, which makes clear that there *never was* a possibility that the computer could be expected to synchronize while three-quarters-of-a-million spectators, including a gaggle of VIP's surrounding the launch site, watched. No reasonable observer could be expected to arrive at any other conclusion.

A similar embarrassment occurred when the generally successful and very high priority cruise missile flight test program was visited by the Secretary of Defense and, of course, an appropriate entourage. On this occasion, not one but two of the expensive missiles struggled a few hundred yards and then plunged into the ocean like wounded ducks. . .proving once again that having a reserve test item with which to guarantee success only insures the extent of the disaster (the Principle of Replication of Failures).

A similar series of events encountered some years ago during the development of still another cruise missile, the Snark, led during that period to common reference to "the Snark-infested waters" around Cape Canaveral. Clearly, hardware exhibits an unfriendliness toward managers which is exceeded only by its innate sense of timing.

That this antagonistic behavior applies equally badly to hardware encountered in everyday life is suggested by the law promulgated by René Augustine, then age 14, which concerns travelers in automobiles in unfamiliar environs: "Attempting to read a roadmap while driving causes all traffic lights to turn green."

Headquarters review team arrives.

Chapter 4

Impending Disaster

The Reality of the Fantasy Factor

We're really gonna get 'em this season.
Last year we were too overconfident.

Greg Augustine, Age 15

The annoying trickle of schedule slippages which had been suffered had, it must be reported, grown to avalanche proportions. The top 40 percent of the engineers had already been reassigned from the project to work on the full-time audit team which was seeking to discover why the project was falling behind schedule. Master schedules were now being reissued on a weekly basis and updated hourly. Even the effort to find a method to accurately estimate schedules was, unfortunately, running late. It seemed that the 99-percent-complete point had been reached in no time at all, but that last 1 percent was taking forever. As it turned out, this was a problem of some long standing. However, things began finally to move forward when the workforce received the threat of help from headquarters.

In 1798, Eli Whitney contracted to deliver 10,000 muskets to the Continental Army within 28 months. As things worked out, he delivered them in 37 months, or in about one-third more time than had been anticipated.

In 1978, a number of new systems were delivered to the U.S. military forces by major defense contractors. On the average, according to the reports submitted to the Congress, these systems were delivered in about one-third more time than had been anticipated. In fact, the only thing that appears to be on schedule is the compliance with Law Number IX, which deals with cost growth.

The fraction "one-third" seems to have scientific significance in determining the schedule error associated with predicting major program events. Some say the correct number is actually more nearly equal to one over *pi*, which may explain why the Indiana Legislature in 1897 came within a few votes of declaring *pi* to equal exactly 3.2.*
The data shown in Figure 31 are derived from a large number of

---

*Actually, things might have been worse: it is also stated in *Facts and Fallacies* by C. Morgan and D. Langford that the Indiana General Assembly has been said to have decided that same year to make *pi* equal 4.

Accuracy of Projecting Accomplishment Date for Major Milestones

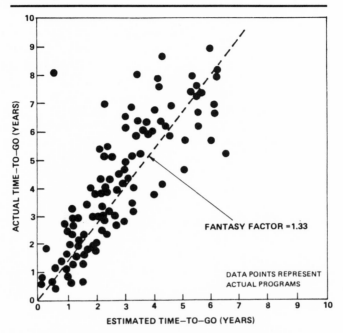

Figure 31   Like cost, the prediction of schedule involves uncertainties and risks. When the time actually required to complete a task is compared with the time which had originally been projected, a quite predictable correction factor can be empirically derived.

official schedule estimates predicting when various milestones, such as first flight, first delivery, etc., will occur. These data, in turn, form the basis for the Law of Unmitigated Optimism, which, in turn, defines the concept of the "Universal Fantasy Factor":

Any task can be completed in only one-third more time than is currently estimated.

(LAW NUMBER XXIII)

Unfortunately, as those familiar with Zeno's Paradox will recognize, each time a program's schedule is reviewed it will be found that only three-fourths of the planned work will have actually been accomplished, and so on ad infinitum, verifying the impossibility of completing anything.

It is a fundamental property of human character to be able to believe in all earnestness, after having missed 22 consecutive monthly schedules, that there is no reason whatsoever to question that the next month's schedule can be met. Denver Broncos defensive coach Joe Collier, recognizing such human failings, approaches the resulting problem in a head-on fashion: "Our goal is five missed tackles a week," he says. This latter condition was in fact approached in the case of the upper-left-hand data point in Figure 31 whereby the manager's official estimate was that his program was eight months from completion when in fact another eight years were required. Presumably this manager is now somewhere writing books on program management. Yogi Berra summarized the situation eloquently: "It isn't over till it's over," he noted with his usual sagacity.

The vice president and general manager of Boeing's 767 division may have had this law in mind, if he was referring to the fraction of *work* previously accomplished, when he remarked, as reported in *Aerospace Daily*, that the 767 "is further ahead at the half-way point than any new airliner program in Boeing history."

Similar reassurance was once offered to the Defense System Acquisition Review Council, the senior acquisition body in the Pentagon, by a manager of a troubled program who promised, "Even though we have fallen behind on the engine development, I feel confident that we will have an engine there for the first flight." As it happened, this turned out to be one of his few correct predictions.

It was only later that it was realized he was an adherent to the James J. Walker school of management: "If you're there before it's over, you're on time!"

Little consolation can be derived from the fact that nearly all programs report "99 percent schedule compliance." This generally means that every weekly letter report in two years has been submitted on time. . .and only the hardware deliveries have fallen hopelessly behind schedule.

Seemingly the last frontier of hope for that body of managers who lead multiyear programs which invariably miss each individual cumulative deadline by "only a few days" lies in participation in the efforts to explore the solar system. By a happy coincidence of planetary kinematics, a *day* on Venus is actually longer than a *year* on Venus. . . making it exceedingly difficult to continually miss deadlines by the proverbial "few days." A few years, yes; a few *days*, no.

If there is a single causal thread in the web of program slippages, it would seem to be that plans are too often made on the basis that nothing in the future will ever go wrong—a "success-oriented" plan, in the vernacular. And if nothing will ever go wrong, there is no need to provide resources such as time, funds, manpower, or facilities for contingencies. The problem is, of course, that something always does go wrong. Will Rogers probably never met Murphy.

The above law is thus seen to address the accuracy of predicting how long it will take to reach any particular milestone in a development program's life. A different law addresses the overall trend of increasing time required actually to prosecute a development program.

Nonetheless, when it comes to schedule adherence, everything seems to be relative. Relatively bad.

Certain Uncertainty

> *It seems to me that no soothsayer*
> *should be able to look at*
> *another soothsayer without laughing.*
> **Cicero to Roman Senate**

If schedule problems have been proving to be resilient, cost control problems are proving to be utterly impossible. But now having solved the problem of schedule prediction once and for all, the search for new management tools shifts to cost estimation. This leads to the next immutable law which explains why one professional football coach, after being given an unlimited budget by the club's owner, was accused before the season had even begun of overspending it.

Two types of uncertainty plague most major programs: known-unknowns and unknown-unknowns. The known-unknowns, such as the composition of the moon's surface at the exact location of the first Apollo landing, can be accommodated and a program planned which minimizes the likelihood of their occurrence and hedges against their consequences. The second category, the unknown-unknowns, cannot be specifically identified in advance, but their existence can be predicted with every bit as much confidence as insurance companies place in actuarial statistics. An example of the latter category of unknown is the lightning that struck Apollo XII shortly after its launch on the way to the moon. Somehow, in every major program, "lightning" strikes *somewhere*. It cannot be predicted *where* it will strike, only that it *will* strike. But, unfortunately, the budgeting system used in defense planning has not, at least not until recently, permitted the recognition of such contingencies and thus the provision of "lightning rods." This was in part due to the presumed vulnerability of so-called management "reserves" to congressional budget cutting, and partly due to optimistic bids engendered in cost-reimbursable competitive contract award environments. But those involved in the process of estimating would be well advised to heed the words of John Gay, "Lest man suspect your tale untrue, keep probability in view."

To illustrate the perversity of nature insofar as it seeks to disrupt the best planned research and development projects, a picture may in fact be worth a thousand words. In Figure *32*, an aerial photo of the site of

Figure 32 *High-lighting an unfortunate coincidence in terminology, the large blow-down wind tunnel shown in the upper left-hand corner of the figure was destroyed when it was inadvertently over-pressured.*

a large NASA wind tunnel, can be seen, in the upper left hand corner, an explosion's effects are observable — the tunnel destroyed, only a pile of heavy pipes left, all in the vicinity of where the tunnel had been, *except for one large section of pipe.* For some reason it chose to fly over the entire building complex and land on the only automobile within sight.

In the words of Robert Burns, "The best laid schemes 'o mice and men gang aft a-gley."

The need to recognize uncertainty when making cost estimates is not an altogether new problem. On March 27, 1794, for example, the Congress authorized building six large frigates to form the backbone of the U.S. Navy. The War Department first began to lay the keels seventeen months later, shortly after which cost overruns and schedule slippages caused the program to be cut back to three ships. Further, the problem is not endemic to any one side of the Potomac. In 1972 the U.S. Senate proposed constructing a new office building

Predicting Program Cost (R&D Plus Procurement)

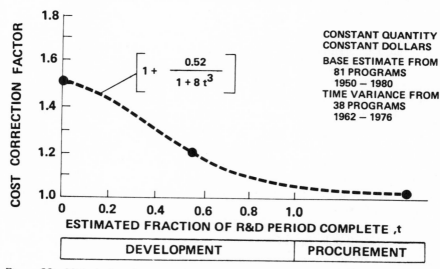

Figure 33   *Historical evidence can be used to determine the correction factor which if used, at least in the past, would have dramatically improved upon the otherwise generally poor cost- estimating track record.*

— hardly an overwhelming challenge of technological uncertainty — at a cost of 48-million dollars. The cost of a stripped-down version of the building soon became 137.7-million dollars. Senator John Chafee notes that this is a mere ten times the cost of the Louisiana Purchase.

Abundant evidence indicates that it is not human nature to learn from well-documented history, but rather to repeat it. The Great Mahaiwe Bank of Great Barrington, Massachusetts recently discovered this when a check written (presumably by a program manager) in payment for a book titled *How to Balance Your Budget* had to be returned due to insufficient funds.

The unchallenged record for abysmal performance goes to a mercifully unspecified missile production program of the mid-1980's reported by the Rand Corporation as having suffered an overrun for a fixed quantity of items variously estimated as between 540 and 1370 percent (corrected, of course, for inflation).

Performance, or rather the lack of performance, of this magnitude is difficult to dismiss merely with the vagaries of probability. Rather, it suggests some association with the Growth Companies of industry that, to everyone's detriment, espouse the motto, "Bid 'em low; watch 'em grow."

Although many more sophisticated ways of predicting program costs are available were one in fact to use them, the cost-estimating correction factor presented in Figure 33 would, in the aggregate, have eliminated overruns on defense programs during the recent decade had it been available and applied. But actions like that could destroy one's bad reputation.

It should be noted that when the data in Figure 33 are in fact applied, the decisionmaker will undoubtedly have been misinformed as to what fraction of the program is actually complete. This distortion has already been compensated for in Figure 33 using Law Number XXIII.* Caution is, of course, in order with respect to the delegation of authority for the management of the contingency funds thus determined, lest Parkinson's Law exert itself and costs rise to match the accessible funds.

In order to better the record of program cost estimators of the past few decades, it will, therefore, be necessary to work twice as hard, to be twice as smart, and to recognize unknown-unknowns. Fortunately, this is not difficult. All of which leads to the Law of Inestimable Consequences:

The most unsuccessful three years in the education of cost estimators appears to be fifth-grade arithmetic.

(LAW NUMBER XXIV)

An advisor to a recent President expressed the view that there should be two requirements met before anyone becomes an economics reporter. First, he ought to have taken a basic economics course; second, he ought to have passed it. It is suspected that too many cost analysts have as their principal credential that they once won an award in fifth grade entitled "Most Enthusiastic in Arithmetic." Simply stated, the prevailing cost-estimating practices are resulting in a record whereby the average estimator has predicted eleven of the last two underruns.

At least our cost control record offers a lot of potential for improvement.

---

*Figure 33 has been updated since the publication of prior editions of "Augustine's Laws" and is based on a larger data sample which reflects somewhat improved performance in the recent decade.

Buying Time

Ever forward. But slowly.
Gebhard von Blucher

The program, in spite of reorganization, promotion, and resolution of the cost and schedule estimation problems, seems inexplicably to be descending further and further into a morass. The solution appears to be to once again revise the schedule so as to save money. But debate breaks out over the following question: "In which direction should the schedule be revised?" In this instance, it was simply a matter of making the wrong mistake.

It is widely recognized that if programs are stretched out *ad infinitum* their costs, even in noninflated dollars, will increase substantially. Conversely, as *production* programs are accelerated within limits, their costs often decrease due to the efficiencies attendant to higher rates of throughput. This is presumably no more than a restatement of the observation that most existing production programs are operating at far from an optimal rate.

Correspondingly, if stretching the schedule increases the cost of *development* programs, then it follows that accelerating the schedule must *decrease* the cost. Right?

Wrong.

An examination of the data in Figure 34 reveals, first, that there are precious little data on programs which have been accelerated and, second, that not only does stretching a *development* program increase cost but *so does accelerating it*. Somehow the status quo, whatever that may be, seems to be the best of all possible worlds. Or at least the most comfortable.

The argument goes that *once a schedule is established*, accelerating is disruptive, may demand overtime, increases the strain on facilities and exacerbates concurrency risks. Decelerating it, on the other hand, increases the cumulative effect on fixed costs and introduces inefficiencies associated with operating with a noncritical mass. Although many decry prolonged schedules and plea for acceleration, the limited record available suggests that *for established development programs*, accelerating, as decelerating, produces one predictable consequence: the contractor will send a bill.

Clearly some additional phenomenon is at work.

Schedule Changes: One Positive Effect

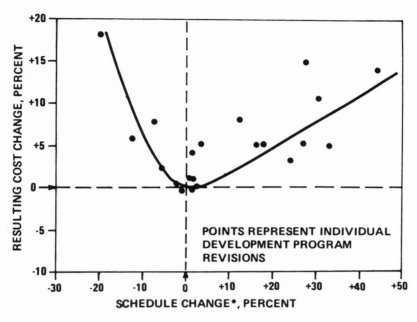

Figure 34   Although evidence relating the impact of schedule changes on cost is sparse, that which does exist indicates that accelerating or decelerating the schedule of an established development program *has the same impact on cost. It increases.*

The Law of Economic Unipolarity summarizes these empirical results*:

The only thing more costly than stretching the schedule of an established development program is accelerating it, which is itself the most costly action known to man.

(LAW NUMBER XXV)

---

*The specific formulation of Law XXV is attributed to a Colorado local newspaper which noted in a news column, in the heat of the commercial nuclear power debate, "Plutonium is even more dangerous than Americum, which itself is the most dangerous substance known to man."

So Simple It Can't Be Trusted

If rats are experimented on,
they will develop cancer.
Morton

The day of reckoning crashes on the scene with a suddenness and a finality that astonishes even the most confirmed pessimists, i.e., the headquarters independent cost-analysts. The event that brings all this about is the sudden appearance of TEST RESULTS. This dread product suffers from the fact that Mother Nature does not seem to respond to the modern management and marketing techniques which proved so successful in the early proposal- writing days. . . which themselves now seem to be merely a distant dream. Even such tried and true methods as declaring the flight which was "prematurely terminated" by the crash on takeoff as being 80% successful (successful checkout, successful start-up, successful taxi, and successful ground run all before the disastrous lift-off phase) no longer seemed to work. In this case the problem was attributed to a static firing of a cantankerous rocket motor... termed in the press release a "successful destructive test." But a consensus begins to emerge as to what should be done to extricate the program from the jaws of the testers while at the same time recovering some much-needed funding. The solution: reduce the amount of testing.

This law concerns the testing of new products and reflects a view expounded by Casey Stengel, late of the New York Yankees, and apparently shared by baseball managers and program managers alike: "I've had no experience with that sort of thing," he said, "and *all* of it has been bad."

Were one to examine the relationship between the amount of testing that is required of a newly developed item and the complexity of that item, it might not be unreasonable to expect that the less complex the product the less testing it requires. That is, an anvil might be expected to require less testing than a new automobile. If, for example, a chart were made showing the number of flight tests of various missile systems against some measure of their complexity, the

Relationship of Missile Complexity (Cost) and
Number of Flight Tests Required

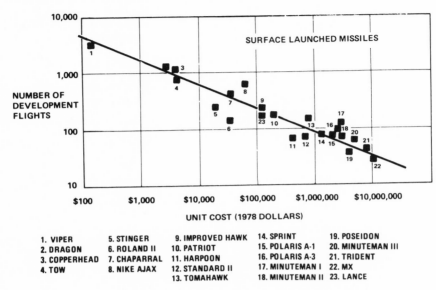

1. VIPER   5. STINGER   9. IMPROVED HAWK   14. SPRINT   19. POSEIDON
2. DRAGON   6. ROLAND II   10. PATRIOT   15. POLARIS A-1   20. MINUTEMAN III
3. COPPERHEAD   7. CHAPARRAL   11. HARPOON   16. POLARIS A-3   21. TRIDENT
4. TOW   8. NIKE AJAX   12. STANDARD II   17. MINUTEMAN I   22. MX
                                 13. TOMAHAWK   18. MINUTEMAN II   23. LANCE

Figure 35   Very simple products often require literally thousands of test articles. Very complex items require very little system test hardware.

two parameters would presumably be directly related, and the trend thereby observed would show a *direct* correlation, i.e., a line sloping *upward* to the right. Such a plot is presented in Figure 35, based on the assumption that unit cost is a not unreasonable surrogate measure of "complexity." It is seen that, in keeping with the now well-established implausibility principle of the development process, the correlation is *not* direct but rather is inverse, with the line sloping *downward* to the right exactly as should have been unexpected in the first place. Thus, one finds that the amount of testing needed *decreases* as an item becomes more complex, providing still another motivation for designers to avoid simplicity and at the same time reduce the likelihood of having the failings of their equipment exposed during testing.

The amount of testing required seems to be more nearly explainable in terms of tradition than in terms of any technical rationale. One suspects that the testers may have taken quite broadly the instruction to test the system. Relatively simple unguided artillery projectiles somehow demand literally thousands of test rounds, whereas a new intercontinental ballistic missile needs only a few handfuls of test flights to demonstrate its adequacy. Thus, the less complex the system, the more testing it requires, a consequence of which forms the basis of the Augustine-McKinley* Law of Complicational Simplicity:

Truly simple systems are not feasible because they require infinite testing.

(LAW NUMBER XXVI)

The data in the figure can be extrapolated to determine that it will be impossible to test systems costing *more* than one-trillion dollars since that cost corresponds to the point on the graph for a single test. The Space Shuttle lies close to this trend based on its four-flight development program and one-billion-dollar-plus price tag. The interpretation, however, may reside in the fact that when a system becomes so complex as to cost, say, 3-trillion dollars a copy (corresponding on the graph to one-half of a flight test) it will always fail midway through its mission.

A very useful "inverse" corollary exists to the above law. It will be noted that when the number of flight tests which are planned in a missile development program is *known*, one may use the curve in Figure 35 to *predict the unit cost* of the item in question! This, in contrast with the more conventional and more comprehensive manner of projecting unit costs, requires only a few manseconds of unskilled labor. Furthermore, it produces results that compare quite favorably in terms of accuracy with the official cost estimates for most programs during the past two decades. In the sample examined during this investigation, the above-mentioned fast-track pricing technique produces an estimate of unit cost which in 40 percent of the cases is within plus or minus one-third of the correct value. The official cost estimation record in recent years is 50 percent within one-third of the true value...a not altogether dissimilar result. Furthermore, the present method not only overestimates the cost about half the time — a phenomenon foreign to the official computation techniques — but also reduces the danger of one's becoming lost inside a computer.

The technique, although powerful, is unfortunately highly brittle and suffers from the consequences of a form of the Heizenberg

---

*Charles H. McKinley, Vice President, Vought Aeronautics, and former Assistant Director of Defense Research and Engineering in the Pentagon.

principle. Specifically, the technique's continued viability depends on test planners not communicating with cost estimators and thence biasing the test programs they construct in a fashion which contaminates their value as cost indicators. However, this should not be a difficulty since test planners seldom talk to anyone else anyway.

The Law of Diminished Returns

The mountains will be in labor,
and a ridiculous mouse will be brought forth.

Horace, 8 B.C.

An examination of the modest production rates being projected leads the struggling manufacturer to complain, paraphrasing Will Rogers' words, that "everyone says something must be done . . . but this time it looks like it might be us." Nonetheless, having reduced testing, halved the quality assurance effort, assigned more lawyers to the project than engineers, eliminated the data package, and even reduced the increase that had been provided in the marketing budget, nothing seems to remain for our tortured program but to save money by slowing the rate at which the product itself is to be built. Surely this will save a great deal of money. Hopefully, it will also reduce the budget inroads being made by other programs, managed less well, that continually seek funds to cover their overruns.

The path of least resistance in allocating scarce production funds among an abundance of competing producers seems to be to build at least some of everything, an approach which can be thought of as the minimum noise solution. The problem, of course, is that the greater the variety of items produced, the fewer, for a fixed budget, of each type of item that can be afforded. Thus, it follows that everything is produced at its least efficient rate because of the small quantities involved. The managers of starved factories attempting to produce on such a basis will find special meaning in the words of former San Francisco Giants manager Dave Bristol, who, paraphrasing Gene Kirby of the Montreal Expos, advised his sagging team, "There'll be two busses leaving the hotel for the ballpark tomorrow. The two o'clock bus will be for those of you who need a little extra work. The empty bus will be leaving at five o'clock."

That the above tendency of production to stabilize at its least efficient rate nonetheless applies is verified in Figure 36. This figure illustrates the actual production rate for a variety of hardware items as compared with their minimum economical rate (generally defined as the output resulting from usage of the respective factories on a minimal one-shift, five-day per week basis). The further a program

146

Assessment of Success in Achieving Efficiency
Through Increased Production Rate

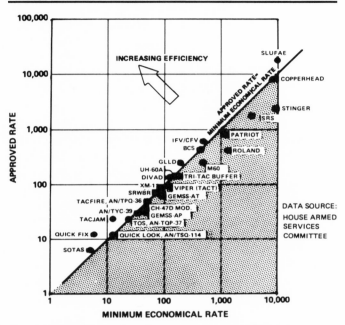

Figure 36   For every production line there is a minimum efficient output rate below which the rhythm of the line is lost and excess capacity and concomitant inefficiency prevail. Most production programs in recent years have been operating on the threshold of this throughput precipice.

moves away from the shaded region in the figure, the more efficient becomes factory operation. Operation *within* the shaded region is generally uneconomical. Yet, as is seen, nearly all programs hover menacingly along the cliff of the shaded region. . .assuring that the factory operates not on a learning curve but more nearly on a forgetting curve.

The problem is exacerbated by the already discussed commonplace error whereby production costs are underestimated... which, when compounded with the inevitable externally imposed budget cuts, causes further reductions in output and factory usage; which, in turn, causes production to "move further up the learning curve" due to the smaller quantities built; which then generates an attendant increase in unit production cost; which thereby requires a further decrease in production rates; which. . . .

Where does all this end? It seems to end when the available funds are stretched to their utmost limit in supporting the maximum number of projects, each at its marginally inefficient rate. Thus, another natural (perhaps unnatural) law seems to have been discovered which has all along been at the root of the well-recognized dilemma whereby each factory invariably seems to be struggling to stay afloat, from an efficiency standpoint, independent of substantial increases or decreases in the overall national availability of funds for production. The Law of Marginal Survival explains the loss in total real output due to inefficiency when an ever-greater variety of underfunded programs is pursued:

The more one produces, the less one gets.

(LAW NUMBER XXVII)

The military aircraft production program in one recent year serves as an unfortunate example. During the year examined, itself not a particularly atypical year, production consisted of fully 20 different types of fixed- and rotary-wing aircraft, of which 11 enjoyed a production rate of 12 aircraft or less per year.

By such conditions we get our enemies right where they want us.

Seeking To Profit
from One's Inexperience

> *Another such victory over the*
> *Romans and we are undone.*
> **Plutarch**

At this juncture, with disaster lurking in all quarters, par-
ticularly in the southeast corner of the contractor's profit-
and-loss statement, the government's program manager
examines a procurement practice similar to one once
referred to by an executive of the Lockheed Corporation as
"You bet your company." The underlying logic is based on
the premise that if there is not enough production to
support one contractor efficiently, it is then necessary to
introduce a second contractor to enhance competition and
thereby increase efficiency. This is much akin to trying to
leap deep chasms in two bounds. Nonetheless, this is
exactly what the government manager of our Grim Fairy
Tale elects to do. As the saying goes among development
contractors faced with second source competition, "If
someone shows you a gun and asks for money, he is not
necessarily trying to sell you the gun." Under such cir-
cumstances the underdog quickly becomes the overdog...
and the contractors become inextricably engaged in a form
of combat from which they will be separated only when
"debt do us part." Presented with such a dilemma, the
incumbent contractor in turn does the only honorable thing;
he inserts some fine print into the contract. By now the
contractor is no longer seeking any cheese. . .he just wants
out of the trap.

Certainly there is nothing more sacred to most industrialists than the
competitive foundation of the Free Enterprise system. . .except, of
course, the opportunity for a sole source award.

Among the most effective means of controlling cost while achieving
superior product performance is to exploit competition among several
potential suppliers. But even competition must be applied carefully, or
unwanted results occur. Consider, for example, the practice occasionally used in the past of awarding the production contract for a

149

Effect of Competition on Unit Price

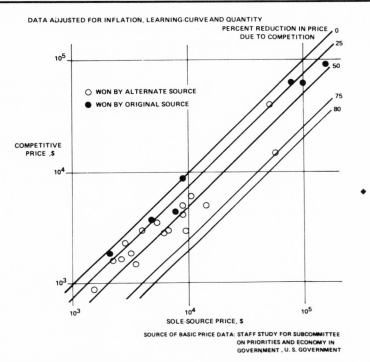

Figure 37 *Competitive procurements have, in general, resulted in price reductions on the order of 25 percent. . . but there are other prices to be considered as well.*

newly developed system to whoever is the low bidder. This has the unquestioned advantage of driving down bid prices. . . and the disadvantage of sometimes creating a producer which has a convenient degree of optimism in pricing, coupled with a total lack of familiarity with the hard-earned lessons of how one actually goes about building the product in question. . . lessons which were at least partially learned over years of agonizing effort by the developer. Upon the award of such a competitive, often fixed-price contract, the ecstasy of the marketing department is generally exceeded only by the foreboding of the finance department. . . which, in turn, is surpassed only by the eager anticipation of the legal department. Worse yet, the winner is often the type of company that, if given a contract to teach a frog to swim, would probably end up drowning the frog.

Will Rogers could have been alluding to the use of competitive breakout procurements *soon after development is completed* when he remarked, "Claremore, Oklahoma, is just waiting for a high-tension line so they can go ahead with locating an airport."

In the words of John Ruskin a century ago, "It's unwise to pay too much, but it is worse to pay too little. When you pay too much, you lose a little money—that is all. When you pay too little, you sometimes lose everything, because the thing you bought was incapable of doing the thing it was bought to do. The common law of business balance prohibits paying a little and getting a lot—it can't be done. If you deal with the lowest bidder, it is well to add something for the risk you run. And if you do that, you will have enough to pay for something better."

The data in Figure 37 verify that major *bid* price reductions are indeed obtainable by placing a number of potential producers in competition for an item developed by one specific contractor. This figure does not, however, examine whether the *winning* bidder was

The Ability of an Established Producer to Win a Breakout Competition

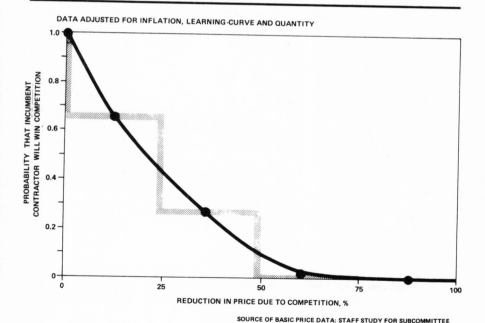

DATA ADJUSTED FOR INFLATION, LEARNING-CURVE AND QUANTITY

y-axis: PROBABILITY THAT INCUMBENT CONTRACTOR WILL WIN COMPETITION

x-axis: REDUCTION IN PRICE DUE TO COMPETITION, %

SOURCE OF BASIC PRICE DATA: STAFF STUDY FOR SUBCOMMITTEE ON PRIORITIES AND ECONOMY IN GOVERNMENT, U.S. CONGRESS

Figure 38   In cases where tooling costs are relatively high, production volume low, or the "data packge" telling how to build an item incomplete, competition for production is usually impractical. The attempt to force competition in such instances increases the tendency for the least qualified producers to win programs which they are incapable of executing.

152

ever actually able to manufacture a useful and reliable end product at the bid price—or, for that matter, any other price. That is not to suggest that when problems do occur there is insufficient blame to be shared by all the program's participants: winners, losers, and even innocent bystanders. The original developer, which in all likelihood itself underestimated the cost at the outset of the development, generally takes the viewpoint expressed by semanticist and senator S.I. Hayakawa: "We should keep it. We stole it fair and square." Or, as Johnny Rutherford was quoted as saying after winning the 1980 Indianapolis 500, "I honestly didn't cheat any more than anyone else." This same concept has led an occasional development contractor to graciously offer to reduce the cost of a financially beleaguered development program by altogether eliminating the data package! This is, of course, the corporate equivalent of two birds in the hand being worth *one* in the bush. In Br'er Rabbit's words, *"Please don't throw me into the briar patch!"*

Figure 38 examines the data in Figure 37 in a slightly different fashion. It indicates that the greater the winner's price reduction relative to the developer's original price, the less likely is the *developer* of the item in question to be the winning bidder. It appears that an intimate knowledge of the task to be performed is a nearly insurmountable handicap. But it must be noted in fairness that some companies do in fact win intensely competed defense contracts — whereas others merely go on to be successful.

There *must* be a message in here somewhere. Perhaps the prior participants in the program simply suffer from being grossly experienced. Or perhaps the incumbent is merely a victim of George Ade's theory that "Anybody can win, unless there happens to be a second entry."

Several interpretations of this phenomenon of the loose cannon, in the form of a marginally qualified, low-balling bidder, on the deck of the breakout procurement process are possible. One of these is expressed, with apologies to Alexander Pope, in the Law of Incipient Disaster (which is also known by some as the Law of Conservation of Misery):

Fools rush in where incumbents fear to bid.
(LAW NUMBER XXVIII)

Shakespeare in *Richard III* alludes to this problem, if not as it plagues the procurement process:

. . . the world is grown so bad
That wrens make prey where eagles dare not perch.

The net impact of unknowledgable bidders in major fixed-price competitions is thus, to borrow from another context an expression of Irving Bluestone, Vice President of the United Auto Workers, "somewhat analogous to that of the cross-eyed discus thrower: he seldom comes out ahead, but he sure does keep the crowd alert."

Similarly, it was this law that a military aviator, with whom the author once had the privilege of flying, apparently had in mind when he added to the caution and warning stickers that traditionally abound in the cockpits of modern rotary-wing aircraft, the following hand-lettered admonition: "Caution. This helicopter built by the lowest bidder."

Sometimes it is best simply to leave bad enough alone.

The Manager of the Year

When the going gets tough, everyone leaves.
Lynch's Law

*It is, in our ever-deteriorating program, becoming in-
creasingly conspicuous that many of the participants are
filling jobs for which they are ill-suited. A decision is
therefore made to shift jobs among the members of the
workforce in order to afford everyone a fresh start. This
turbulence is worsened by the sudden appearance of
hordes of head-hunters, referred to in more dignified circles
as executive search firms, all seeking to precipitate a game
of musical chairs. . . with commissions. There exists a law
which addresses the problem of management turnover
which is premised on the possibility that most managers
think they know their capacity, but simply pass out before
they reach it.*

Certainly, one of the greatest impediments to that fundamental
precept of management referred to as accountability is the rapid
turnover of individuals holding leadership positions. Government
program managers in the acquisition process, for example, hold their
jobs an average of only 30 months. Even this is a substantial improvement over the situation which existed just a few years ago when
in 1965 such managers retained their jobs an average of only 15
months. Over the last two decades the tenure of Secretaries of Military
Departments and the Secretary of Defense as a group has been no
better, also averaging about 30 months. There is, of course, the
perspective taken by one senior military officer, "There is no problem
with rotating people as long as they aren't doing anything anyway!"
The consequences of this anonymity in responsibility once prompted
an aggrieved Lyndon Johnson to remark, in response to a question by
a reporter as to why he had not fired the individual who had scuttled
one of the President's favorite programs, "Fire him? Hell, I can't even
find him."

Could it be possible that so important a management tenet as
leadership stability and accountability has been totally overlooked in
managing our nation's defense affairs? No, there is reason for optimism. Consider the following newspaper article quoting senior Navy
managers: "By constantly changing our. . . director every two or three

155

years, we have destroyed continuity." "If you had a million-and-a-half dollar business, would you want to change bosses every three years for someone who didn't have any experience?" "Most directors come right from sea duty to this job, and it can take a full year to get to know the ropes. . . .How many people in the Navy do you think know things like scheduling problems?"

Encouraging indeed: the problem *is* recognized. Presumably an article from the pages of *The Wall Street Journal* discussing the management of an important new Navy fighter aircraft, or perhaps even a new shipbuilding program? Alas, the article is from the sports page of *The Washington Post*, addressing the decision reached a few years ago to stop rotating individuals through the position of Athletic Director at the Naval Academy. At least we have our priorities in perspective.

Gilbert Fitzhugh, Chairman of the Blue Ribbon Defense Panel of the late 1960's, stated the situation in the following terms: "Everybody is somewhat responsible for everything, and nobody is completely responsible for anything." A two-star general once commented in an outburst of candor in response to a question as to how he was going to work his program out of a seemingly untenable position into which it had descended, "Perhaps a miracle will happen, or else maybe I'll get transferred!"

Dr. Ray Cline, the former Deputy Director of the Central Intelligence Agency, reminds that the essence of planning is to be nearby when successes occur. . . and far away when disaster strikes.

This problem of personnel turbulence, troublesome in virtually all management situations, is particularly acute in the case of major research and development undertakings. Consider the fact that studies of the frequency of reference to technical articles held in libraries, and of the change of content of course catalogs in the scientific department of universities, indicate that the half-life of many technologies is today only about ten years.*

Paraphrasing this inconsistency as once pointed out by the *Armed Forces Journal*, we are attempting to develop major new systems with ten-year technology, eight-year programs, a five-year plan, three-year people, and one-year dollars.

Attendant to each change of management there is likely to be an instant "virtual" cost increase as the new leadership offloads blame on

---

*After considerable deliberation and selected consultations, the author has concluded not to generate a law pointing out the connection between the scarcity of female engineers and the fact that in most engineering disciplines one is professionally middle-aged by age thirty.

Personnel Stability in Acquisition Process

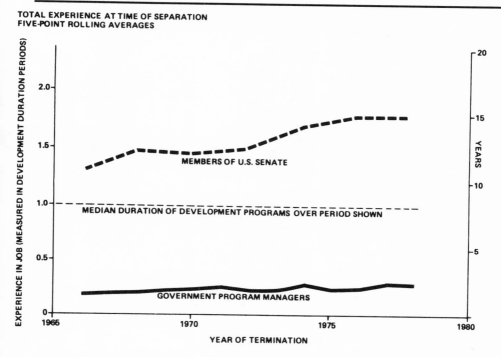

TOTAL EXPERIENCE AT TIME OF SEPARATION
FIVE-POINT ROLLING AVERAGES

Figure 39   The turnover period for program management is very short in relation to the period of time required for the completion of major development undertakings.

the old management and builds shelter for itself. A brief study of the System Acquisition Reports (SARs), which present quarterly cost data to the Congress on all major systems, reveals a strong correlation between changes in management and jumps in projected cost immediately after the changeover.

Thus, a long succession of management changes takes place but with seemingly no improvement in results. A discouraged Casey Stengel once canonized this phenomenon in these words: "Two hundred million Americans, and there ain't two good catchers among 'em."

The evidence which underlies Law Number XXIX is presented in Figure 39, wherein the longevity of program managers is compared with the (average) longevity of the programs they manage. As also shown in the figure, the people at the top of the legislative structure experience relatively *little* turnover. These members of the Legislative Branch not infrequently remind witnesses testifying before R&D

hearings that the Congressmen and Senators themselves know more about the history and underlying problems of the programs in question than does the parade of new so-called experts who appear before them year after year with ever-greater enthusiasm and optimism. Sometimes one wonders if perhaps only the names have been changed simply to protect the *guilty*. It is just this dichotomy, aggravated by the very length of the acquisition process, which in fact leads to the Law of Limited Liability:

The problem with the acquisition process is that by the time the people at the top are ready for the answer the people at the bottom have forgotten the question.

(LAW NUMBER XXIX)

Even among executives who believe they are capable of personally dictating the solution to any and all problems, it is still useful to know the questions to the answers.

The Half-Life of a Manager

We have a lot of players in their first year.
Some of them are in their last year.
Bill Walsh, Coach, San Francisco 49ers

A trying time has befallen the senior management of the program. When the subsystems first began failing their tests it had been necessary to take decisive action, such as doubling the size of the contigent to the Paris Air Show. It was thus particularly untimely for all the exhausted managers returning from what is fondly referred to among the initiated as the Paris Death March to discover that costs had run hopelessly out of control and schedules had been slipping at a rate of two days per day (albeit with techniques now clearly established to prevent this regrettable occurrence in the future). Talk of potential catastrophy among the program's participants, both contractor and customer, had become rampant. If only, it was asserted, those who labored so arduously in the trenches had not been suppressed, things would be different. Thus exited the first echelon of management of the program. Good riddance.

Law XXX examines the viewpoint expressed by former Dallas Cowboy guard Blaine Nye: "It's not whether you win or lose that counts," he says, "but who gets the blame." Will Rogers once pointed out with respect to his business pursuits, "It is not the return on my investment that I am concerned about; it is the return of my investment." Perhaps within this philosophy lies the key to refute the rather disappointing thrust of the earlier law which examined management incentives.

Possibly the significant consideration with respect to successful managers is not *what* they keep getting from their job, but rather that they are getting to *keep* their job. This possibility can be readily assessed using Figure 40, which displays the number of years the top executive in the 20 most profitable firms in the United States, in recent years, has been able to hold his job, as a function of the success achieved by that executive in increasing the company's profits. Unfortunately, the results are doubly disappointing. Not only do they fail

Executive Survivability

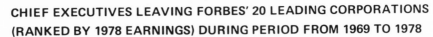

CHIEF EXECUTIVES LEAVING FORBES' 20 LEADING CORPORATIONS
(RANKED BY 1978 EARNINGS) DURING PERIOD FROM 1969 TO 1978

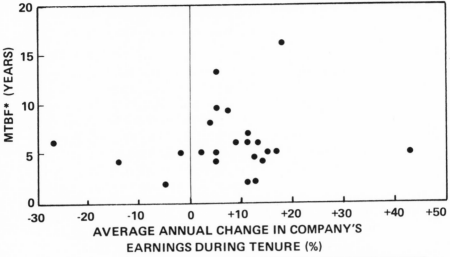

Figure 40   Data which relate longevity of corporate executives to profitability of the firms they lead indicate only very subtle correlations. If any.

to refute Law Number XIII, but worse, they call for still another law, the Law of Infinite Mortality:

> **Executives who do not produce successful results can be expected to hold on to their jobs only about five years. On the other hand, those who do produce effective results can expect to hang on about half-a-decade.**
>
> **(LAW NUMBER XXX)**

It should be possible to fight this form of apathy; but so far it has not been possible to find anyone interested enough to do so. The conclusion of the above law seems to be true over a wide span of profit growth and even over severe profit "retrenchments," as they are gently referred to in stockholder's reports. The correlation coeffient between profit growth and the ability to retain one's job, on a scale where zero is purely random and 1.0 represents perfect correlation, is calculated to be 0.1. The strongest correlation observed between longevity and any other parameter examined is found to be between the first letter in the name of the company and the first letter in the last name of the chief executive; as in "Ford, Henry II."

As Prince Philip put it, "I'm self-employed."

A median survival duration of a little over five years for top executives may seem rather short at first glance.* However, it is really quite good when compared with many other professions, such as, say, coaching football. Many practitioners of this latter art have had fine careers one afternoon! Consider the case of the Washington Redskins coach who, several years ago, was fired at half-time of the first exhibition game; or the situation that developed a few years later when the team had three head coaches in 24 hours. In fact, in pro football it is clearly a liability to be recognized for outstanding performance. Of the last 15 coaches to be honored by the Associated Press as coach of the year, 11 were fired within the next 12 months. As Bum Phillips, coach of the Houston Oilers, notes, "There's only two kinds of coaches, them that's been fired and them that's about to be fired."**

It would seem that to err may in fact be human, but to forgive is, by and large, against company policy. As John McKay, coach of the Tampa Bay Buccaneers, points out, *They're paid to catch the ball.* It can, of course, be asserted that many of the individuals included in the data base of Figure 40 retired or moved on to more important jobs. But it can be equally accurately asserted that many of these individuals were yet relatively young at the time of their departure and already enjoyed some of the best jobs in America.

Nonetheless, there is no need for discouragement, since the incentive system is, in spite of the above evidence, still alive and well: "People who show the best example in their work must receive greater material benefit"—according to a speech . . . before the Supreme Soviet . . . by the Premier . . . of the U.S.S.R. And right here at home it was recently pointed out that "the challenge for American capitalism in the '80s is to bring the entrepreneurial spirit back to America. Depressed areas especially need enormous investment of capital. Individual entrepreneurship can create the new work ethic that is so desperately needed in America. To stimulate that ethic America needs creative financing. . . and I intend to work to create it."

So said Jerry Rubin, Yippie Leader of the 1960's and a defendent in the Chicago Seven trial. . . speaking in the 1970's as a security analyst on Wall Street.

---

* The data sample considered in Figure 40 contains a slight potential bias since the available evidence covers only a ten-year period. The impact of this is to have relatively little effect on the median longevity addressed herein; however, the overall (arithmetic) average longevity would perhaps increase to seven or eight years.

** Phillips has now been fired by Houston.

Anonymity by Committee

It was a turkey.

Dickens

"Something drastic must be done." So spoke the new management after but a few months on the job. Quarterly reviews were already being held on a weekly basis. The program was unmistakably in-extremis. From the viewpoint of the workers the situation had degenerated to one of man exploiting man instead of the other way around, as it had been under the previous management. It seemed that insufficient talent was available to attack the myriad of problems created by the earlier leadership; problems which by now were appearing at a frequency even far surpassing anything that had been hoped by the legal department. The solution was to form everyone into committees. This would permit the focus of more talent on each problem as it arose. Surprisingly, unlike most of the other actions taken by the program's senior management, this one received widespread acclaim among the workforce. As always, there were skeptics who suggested that many of the problems were, under the old system, merely becoming embarrassingly easy to associate with the responsibilities of specific individuals.

It has long been recognized that the formation of a committee is a powerful technique for avoiding responsibility, deferring difficult decisions, and averting blame. . . while at the same time maintaining a semblance of action. It has also long been suspected that committees dealing with difficult and controversial issues generally accomplish little more in terms of resolving the issues than to agree to disagree. . . and establish a follow-up committee.

In the words of Kelly Johnson, the former head of Lockheed's famous Skunk Works, speaking on CBS Television's *Sixty Minutes,* "We're into the era where a committee designs the airplanes. You never do anything totally stupid, you never do anything totally bright. You get an average wrong answer. . .and very expensive."

One example of this phenomenon as it relates to a Congressional conference committee was reported by the media as follows: "On the fiercely lobbied subject of new long-range cargo planes for the Air

Usefulness of Research Reports as Function of Number of Co-authors

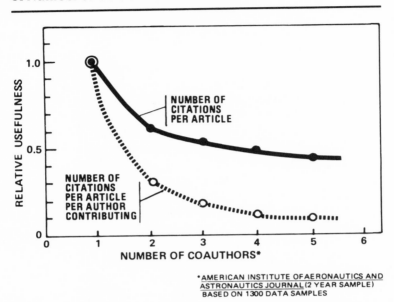

*AMERICAN INSTITUTE OF AERONAUTICS AND
ASTRONAUTICS JOURNAL (2 YEAR SAMPLE)
BASED ON 1300 DATA SAMPLES

*Figure 41   Committees are a very popular management tool in government, in-
dustry, and academia. Measurements of the effectiveness of various size committees
using the number of co-authors of technical articles as a surrogate for committee size
and the number of references to their work as a metric of usefulness do not produce
encouraging findings for committee advocates.*

Force, the conferees opted for the Pentagon's choice of the Lockheed
C-5B. However, they also set aside funds to buy three Boeing 747
aircraft in recognition of the Senate's choice of that plane."

Now who could possibly be better qualified to select the next-
generation military transport than a Congressional committee, and
what better criterion than "in recognition of...?" A consolation award,
apparently.

But these minor albeit widely recognized shortcomings have in no
way hampered the creation of committees. . . much to the joy of
punsters who take pleasure in pointing out such pedantic observations
as "a camel is a horse designed by a committee." And, as might be
suspected, the U.S. Congress is in fact exerting its rightful role of
leadership even in the committee-proliferation arena. . . with the
existence not only of a plethora of congressional committees, but with
the formation of, yes, a *Committee on Committees*. It is the duty of

the Committee on Committees to assign members to other committees, which in turn assign members to the subcommittees of those committees, which in turn, presumably. . . .

Under the Carter Administration it was found that the Federal Government possessed no fewer than 1,175 formal external advisory committees. A review of the utility of these committees (by a committee, undoubtedly) led to the conclusion that all but 16 committees were indispensable.

It turns out to be an extraordinarily challenging undertaking to attempt to quantify the output of committees of various sizes; or, for that matter, of any size. Perhaps it is not simply happenstance that it seems to defy human imagination to identify instances wherein committees have been formed under circumstances which lead to *measurable* contributions. One, admittedly marginal, instance does seem to exist, however, which is an exception to this rule. This is the case of ad hoc "committees" which are created to undertake and report upon scientific research. By making the assumption that the contribution of a given piece of scientific work performed by these committees is somehow measurable in terms of the frequency with which that work is cited by other researchers as they in turn pursue their own work, one can perhaps assess the utility of the *ad hoc* committees themselves. The key assumption is, of course, that the value of a piece of work is proportional to the extent which that contribution is used to assist others in subsequent research. Presumably a work of no value will be relegated forever to the archives; a valuable piece of work, on the other hand, will resurface repeatedly as a building block.

Figure 41 examines research reported by various-size teams of authors in one technical publication, the *American Institute of Aeronautics and Astronautics Journal.* The illustration relates the *relative* frequency with which articles having various numbers of coauthors are cited in the "references" listed in support of later pieces of work by other authors.* It is found, interestingly, that as the number of coauthors increases, the number of citations *per article* decreases. Further, if the number of citations is evaluated *per author* whose time is occupied (asserting, in effect, that each author might,

---

*In an effort to enhance objectivity in measuring worth, instances wherein authors cite their *own* prior work have been eliminated from these data. Agreements to cite each other's work remain unexpurgated! There also remains some statistical risk that articles in the *AIAA Journal* and references cited in the *Journal* may not be totally consistent sets. There appears to be little doubt, however, that the per capita "useful output" as measured herein diminishes significantly as committee size increases.

alternatively, have been doing individual research), the above-mentioned trend is even more striking.* For some reason, articles written by groups of people are of less interest (and value?) to others than articles prepared by a single individual.

Thus, as shown in the figure, the *least* productive committees have several members while the *most* productive "committee" evaluated has but one member. Generalizing, if a committee of 30 is less good than a committee of 10, which is in turn less good than a committee of 1, the Law of Rampant Committeemanship can be derived by extrapolating toward the left the data shown in the figure, with the following result:

The optimum committee has no members.

(LAW NUMBER XXXI)

In this case, at least, less is more. Or, as stated by Hesiod in 700 BC, "Fools, they do not even know how much more is the half than the whole."

Although there is regrettably little evidence to support any projected demise of the committee as a social institution, hope nonetheless springs eternal that the committee problem may be self-healing. L. M. Boyd, the writer, reports for example that the Ultrasaurus, a large dinosaur, had two brains. . . one in its head and the other in its posterior. Boyd concluded that what led to its extinction may in fact have been no less than. . . *committee decisions*. In any event, the notion seems sufficiently promising that it might be worth forming a committee to look into the prospect.

---

* There appears to be no evidence that projects involving multiple authors take less time than those involving single authors. In fact, one *suspects* that the opposite may be true.

Test range photo, courtesy of U.S. Army

Chapter 5

Disaster

For the Want of a Nail

Nuts.
Anthony Clement McAuliffe
Bastogne, 1944

Looking back, the beginning of the end had begun in an unanticipated way. . . with the failure of a solder joint which in turn created what is always referred to as a "flight anomaly." Subsequent to collecting the parts which survived the crash, it was found that the design was in error, parts that had been made did not match the drawings, and the quality control was defective. Aside from this, however, the new management appeared to be regaining control. But the disappointment over the new rash of hardware problems was intense, particularly in view of the flight record which had only recently successfully built up to two strings of one-in-a-row. Unfortunately, morale was not helped at this point by renewed criticism from those who, it will be recalled, months before had pointed out that if the test program had been still further curtailed this sort of failure might not have occurred. It was becoming increasingly apparent that the happiest time on this project had been the period between the contract award and the initiation of work.

For some inexplicable reason, when dealing with a multimillion dollar piece of equipment the part that fails is always a seven-dollar seal, a seventy-cent bolt, or even more likely, a seven-cent solder joint.

The truthfulness of this suspected behavior of hardware is verified by the evidence presented in Figure 42, which examines flight failures occurring in the space program. Each data point represents the loss of a mission due to a booster hardware failure and relates the cost of the hardware launched, excluding payload, to the approximate cost of the item causing the mission to fail. The cost shown is that of the lowest level replaceable unit with which the cause of failure can be associated based on available data, and thus represents a *maximum* cost. In nearly all cases the cause of failure is probably traceable to a far lesser component costing at least an order of magnitude less than shown in the figure. As pointed out in Klipstein's Law, an expensive

171

Being Eaten By The Ducks

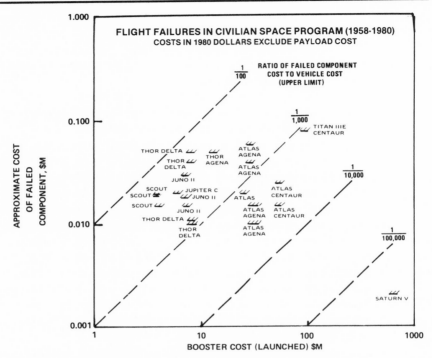

Figure 42   Most test failures of major systems are due to seemingly innocuous faults in components which themselves represent but a small fraction of the cost of the overall system. Extraordinary discipline and attentiveness to detail are thereby demanded in major technical undertakings since hardware is very unforgiving of human failings, no matter how well intended.

"transistor protected by a fast-acting fuse will always protect the fuse by blowing first."

The reason for such behavior is that potential major problems which are identified (and feared) early in a program receive intense scrutiny and are thereby most often averted. It is thus left to one of the literally millions of small elements that comprise a major system and which demand such great personal vigilance and discipline from all levels of workers to fall prey to the unforgiving laws of probability. A poster displayed prominently in many flight operations centers of airports catering to private pilots aptly points out, "Aviation in itself is not inherently dangerous. But to an even greater degree than the sea, it is terribly unforgiving of any carelessness, incapacity or neglect."

This is attested to by, among others, the designer of the tie-down bolts for the original Viking rocket. . .a rocket which to this day holds the world altitude record for static firings. Or the guidance system for the early and errant rocket which came to be known as the world's first ICBM: "Into Cuba by Mistake."

Based upon extensive evidence of the type cited above, the Law of Amplification of Agony can be derived:

One should expect that the expected can be prevented but that the unexpected should have been expected.

(LAW NUMBER XXXII)

The history of aerospace is rife with examples of this phenomenon, many rich with irony as well as agony. The developer of one particular aircraft engine, after suffering a series of highly destructive failures on a test stand due to foreign objects (bolts, washers, small tools) being inadvertently left inside test engines, dictated a procedure whereby prior to each run an inspector would physically enter the inlet of the engine and personally inspect for extraneous objects using a flashlight and thence certify *in writing* that no such objects were to be found. Only then would a test be initiated. As one should expect, however, it was only a short time until still another failure occurred. . . this time due to the inspector's flashlight having been left in the inlet.

Similarly, during the early days of the Standard ARM (Anti-radiation Missile) program, a number of particularly serious flight failures were encountered during combat, setting off a series of investigations ranging from technical assessments to probes into the possibility of sabotage. The culprit? A small safety warning sticker with metalized ink placed on the skin of the missile had been peeling off during flight and neatly passing through the radar fuze!

When, in the development of a new ICBM, it was learned that the data carried over one of the 250 telemetry channels in use was shock-sensitive, a review of channel assignments could reveal *only* one possible happenstance:yes, that channel was carrying the data on the shock environment!

A still more exotic failure was narrowly averted during a critical series of flight tests conducted at the personal direction of the Secretary of Defense to determine whether or not the Patriot air defense missile should be cancelled. Just moments prior to launch of the very first flight, a wild bobcat climbed a power pole at Holloman Air Force Base, some miles from the missile test center at White Sands, suffering an electrifying experience and while so-doing shutting down all range power at the missile site. Had this occurred just seconds later, the missile would have automatically self-destructed for safety reasons due to the loss of ground tracking. Fortunately, in this instance due to a breakdown of the Law of Natural Belligerence, a result of the bobcat having climbed the pole four seconds too soon, the only effect was a delayed program and a number of sets of jangled nerves. If it were somehow possible to obtain a nickel for every dollar lost in such a manner, it might be that no future funding would be required for R&D projects whatsoever — they could become self-sustaining!

On another program, this one in the 1960's, two missile electrical boxes manufactured by different contractors were joined together by a pair of wires which connected into the boxes. Thanks to a particularly thorough preflight check, it was discovered that the wires had been reversed, and instructions were thence sent out for the contractors to correct the problem. It was left to the ensuing postflight failure analysis to reveal that the contractors had indeed corrected the reversed wires as instructed. Except that *both* of them had made the correction. . . proving once again that two wrongs do not make a right.

But the plethora of such stories notwithstanding, the solution now apparently being pursued to the problem of low-cost components causing flight failures warrants questioning. That solution? As previously implied in Law Number IX, simply eliminate all low-cost components by making *every* component a *high*-cost component. As any reasonable marketing manager could point out, such parts are *absolutely failure-proof* and, furthermore, are easily repaired.

To Work or Not To Work. . .

What a time for the roof to leak. Just when it is raining. Not only was the hardware not working in our potentially terminally ill program, but the hardware was actually getting worse with each passing day. Hardware is unable to withstand the pressures of functioning in the world of reality. . . working well on the practice field but failing miserably when the chips are down. And the standard expedient and great American cure-all of throwing money at the problem seemed in this case merely to purchase high reliability that the item in question would not be reliable at all. The words of that esteemed humanist, Snoopy, seemed to apply: "Yesterday I was a dog. Today I'm a dog. Tomorrow I'll probably still be a dog."

But there is still another annoying property exhibited by hardware even after its cost has been established and after its design has been finalized. This is the propensity of hardware to sense when a malfunction would be the *most* harmful. . . and then invariably failing *precisely* at that moment. The subconscious and widespread acceptance of this belief among those engaged in development activities is suggested by the offhand remark of a senior engineer making a report several years ago in the Pentagon at the flight failure investigation of a major space mission. With noticeable satisfaction and no small amount of pride he announced, "We have never had a solder joint fail except for the one during the flight." A generalization of this attitude was once evidenced by a somewhat excited young engineer/marketeer who, in a briefing to the Deputy Director of Defense Research and Engineering on the tactical mobility of his product, blurted out in a moment of candor, "This system is deplorable worldwide." Such remarks would lead one to believe that this type of hardware must be stemming from factories such as the legendary one which was said to be so disorganized that, when it was struck by a tornado, over three-million dollars of improvement was done.

Figure 43 quantifies this intransigent behavior of hardware based on

176

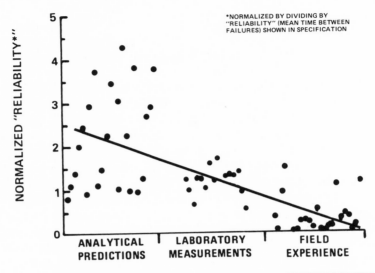

Figure 43 Initial analytical estimates of a system's reliability, as measured by its mean time between failures, have traditionally been several times more favorable than the required value. Actual field experience, on the other hand, has correspondingly been several times less favorable.

a sampling of reliability outcomes actually exhibited by a number of equipment items.* It will be noted from the figure that for each step a given item of hardware moves closer to its intended use, its reliability decreases by a factor of two. In this context, it is observed with regret that, unlike pearls and fine wine, bad news seldom improves with age. In moving from analytical predictions to laboratory tests, for example, mean time between failure (MTBF) deteriorates by a factor of two. In moving from laboratory test to actual field use, the mean time between failure erodes by another factor of two. Fortunately, there is no important program phase beyond "field usage". . . . if there were the data in the figure suggest such a phase might even be characterized by

---

*The data are spaced along the abscissa in a manner which preserves the same sequential order of programs for each phase shown.

a negative MTBF. . . which perhaps is merely a form of what might be a more appropriate measure anyway—some type of MTBW.

It has, of course, often been pointed out with respect to such results (usually by the builders of the hardware in question) that laboratory tests frequently do not involve so severe an environment as is encountered in the real world, or that human-caused failures in actual operation should not be counted at all. These explanations, however, are somewhat hollow in that they leave unexplained what then might be the *purpose* of conducting tests or performing analyses that do *not* relate to the actual circumstances which the beleaguered user of the items in question will have to face. . . or, for that matter, why laboratory tests are not then conducted in a *truly* benign environment so as to free the developer *altogether* from the burdensome nuisance of fixing those failures which are in fact uncovered.

The only possible explanation seems to lie in the fact that either reliability figures are not intended to be assessed in a fashion which relates to what a user can expect or else hardware, although working well under circumstances when it is unimportant, simply does not possess the fortitude to work when it experiences the pressures of the real world. Dismissing the former as being unreasonable, the true explanation must then logically reside in the Law of Hardware Belligerency:

Hardware works best when it matters the least.
(LAW NUMBER XXXIII)

Dr. John Allen, President of General Research Corporation, maintained for a number of years a plot of the trend in reliability of airborne fire-control systems as a function of calendar time. Reliability, that is, as reflected in the design *specifications* for new systems. The improvement in specified mean time between failures of the most advanced systems was truly spectacular, growing at a rate of a factor of ten each decade.

Unfortunately, the same analysis showed that the mean time between failure actually being realized in *operational* units was always simply a fixed number far below the specified values. Apparently some new universal reliability constant, like pi and "e," was at work throughout this period which was undermining the great advancements which were being made in the state-of-the-art of specification writing. Fortunately, recent trends are more encouraging, but it was nonetheless necessary to arrive at the conclusion that airborne electronics are not responsive to enthusiasm.

The consequences of the above law of enduring recalcitrance are exacerbated by the tendency of human managers, when faced with the prospect of a funding shortfall, to eliminate that part of a program which has the least near-term impact, is quite costly, and is not mandatory in terms of demonstrating the so-called fundamental (read "ideal") capability of the system at hand. . . i.e., reliability development and testing. An accurate assessment of such practices is given by Dallas Green, manager of the world champion Phillies, on the heels of his team's fourth straight defeat the following year, as to how they had fallen into their last-place status: "We've earned it," he declared.

The placement of high priority on reliability enhancement is seen to be. . . and perhaps always will be. . . the idea of the future.

Caveat Emptor

I would not join a group
which would have me as a member

Groucho Marx

Having failed to alleviate the ever-growing signs of incipient collapse, top management decides at last to resort to truly dramatic measures. With considerable fanfare it appoints a covey of consultants to undertake The Study. Best of all, at least from the perspective of the program's beleaguered participants, this new episode promises a welcome respite from the day-to-day tribulations of pursuing the project — since further work must now await the consultants' report. Still better, an additional several months of diversion will most assuredly ensue while the program's participants carefully rebuff, one by one, each of the consultants' recommendations and demonstrate why each in turn should not be implemented. And best of all, an unarguably prestigious group of consultants has, in this instance, been assembled. The more exalted the group of consultants, the longer the dismissal process necessarily consumes. Publilius Syrus observed that "Many receive advice, few profit by it." Some consultants will of course assert that their recommendations do have a chance. But then, so did Custer.

A consultant is an individual handsomely paid for telling senior management of problems which senior management's own employees have told the consultant. The consultant offers the advantage of generally having had no first-hand experience in the matters of interest, thereby assuring a clear mind uncluttered by any of the facts.

In the words of former Deputy Secretary of Defense Frank Carlucci, "Task forces are usually led by, if not composed of, people from outside the organization, so they will not be tainted by existing biases. It frequently happens that they are not tainted by any relevant experience, either." But with the day-to-day demands of managing and working (some would say "or") on a project being what they are, it is usually concluded that only an external professional advisor would have readily available the ample time necessary to undertake a study. Individuals more astute than executives who hire advisors might conceivably be distracted by this paradox.

That the conduct of studies must nonetheless be concluded to be an extremely effective management technique is attested by its widespread use. Certainly, only a very powerful tool could enjoy such universal acclaim. The success enjoyed by studies, at least in the case of the defense acquisition process, is shown in Figure 44, which depicts the actual number of such investigations which have been conducted into that much suffering enterprise each year for the past two decades.* An ever-increasing propensity to study is observed, punctuated by the *major* assessments that invariably mark the beginning of each new administration.

Unfortunately, as has been noted, identifying *symptoms* of the maladies that torment the acquisition process is relatively easy; this then forms the body of the canonical study. The task of isolating the problems themselves is more complex and is thus afforded accordingly less attention. Offering *legitimate* solutions proves really difficult — and is, therefore, largely disregarded. But by far the greatest challenge of all, *implementing* solutions, is not the province of either consultants or their studies. Thereby, presumably, deriveth the durability of both.

Selecting advisors and advisory boards to perform studies is a weighty (in gold) matter. Virtually all advisors of course offer impeccable credentials. . .which can easily lead to misinterpretation by the unwary. An advisor may well profess a "diverse background in military and commercial endeavors with a long history of successful projects." That probably means that he was once responsible for coordinating the air support at the Bay of Pigs, and in his salad days performed the market research leading to the Edsel.

It is thus not surprising that performing studies, perhaps the world's second oldest profession, is traditionally demeaned as being susceptible to practice by any individual possessing a briefcase and remaining at least 50 miles from where people know him. There are, fortunately, glaring exceptions to this piece of folklore; but, sadly, these exceptions are exceptions.

Consider the pathology of the canonical study. The first chapter invariably comprises a review of prior studies of the same topic and exhaustive discussion of the reasons why their findings were never implemented. (The growing body of studies in the archives makes this

---

*The author is indebted for the assistance of Richard E. Harris who, in the course of a review of the abovementioned studies, provided the statistical data presented in the figure.

Major Studies of DOD Acquisition Process

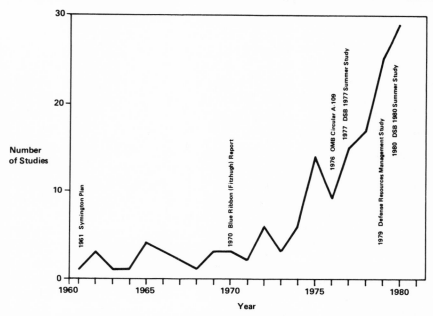

Figure 44   The number of studies of problems in the acquisition process has nearly kept pace with the number of problems in the acquisition process. Each new administration initiates such a study early in its term and thereby gains substantial insight —just in time to be replaced by a successive administration. . .which in turn initiates a sutdy of problems in the early. . ..

an avenue of ever-increasing promise.) The second chapter typically advises improved management accompanied, of course, by a better-motivated workforce bound together in a new organizational structure. The third and final chapter dutifully notes that the problem at hand has, unexpectedly, proven to be even more intractable than originally anticipated — and thus the initiation of three new studies is recommended. As La Rochefoucauld noted years ago, "*Nothing* is given so profusely as advice." It is noteworthy that La Rochefoucauld used the word "profusely" and not the word "freely."

The Law of Analytical Alchemy, germane to the proliferation of studies and advisors, can be stated in its least charitable form as follows:

Hiring advisors to conduct studies can be an excellent means of turning problems into gold: your problems into their gold.

(LAW NUMBER XXXIV)

But a lifetime of providing advice and performing studies does exact its price. The very insulation of their profession from both the hazards and the excitement of hands-on involvement implies that its practitioners must be satisfied with the more vicarious pleasures of their work. Illustrative of this necessity, a recent Army recruiting poster portrayed a grizzled soldier in an airborne division proudly proclaiming, "I hate to jump; I just like to be around the kind of people who do." Lucius Aemilius Paulus, the Roman counsel who was to lead the war against the Macedonians some twenty centuries ago, summarized the situation with more learned gloss:

"I am not one of those who think that commanders ought at no time to receive advice; on the contrary, I should deem that man more proud than wise, who regulated every proceeding by the standard of his own single judgment. What then is my opinion?

"That commanders should be counselled, chiefly, by persons of known talent; by those who have made the art of war their particular study, and whose knowledge is derived from experience; from those who are present at the scene of action, who see the country, who see the enemy; who see the advantages that occasions offer, and who, like people embarked in the same ship, are sharers of the danger. If, therefore, any one thinks himself qualified to give advice respecting the war which I am to conduct, which may prove advantageous to the public, let him not refuse his assistance to the state, *but let him come with me into Macedonia.*"

Occasionally an advisor with a distaste for Macedonia *will* contribute exactly the piece of information or perform precisely the study needed to resolve an otherwise seemingly unsolvable problem. Such cases can generally be characterized as involving advisors or groups of advisors who, first, have hands-on experience in the field of concern; second, are constructive "doers" rather than mere "viewers" (or worse yet, "viewers with alarm"); third, offer a truly independent perspective; and, fourth, are willing to devote the not inconsiderable personal effort demanded to understand the intricacies of the management and technical problems at hand. . .in short, to become engaged. *These* individuals *are* worth their weight in gold. But absent such individuals, together with a sponsor who is *truly* interested in doing something *about* the problem at hand (other, that is, than studying it), it is advisable to give further study to the idea of initiating a study.

Too Late Smart

If it looks like a duck
and if it walks like a duck
and if it quacks, then it's a duck.

Sen. Edward Kennedy

It was a first in the annals of program management: three consecutive months of having received the Golden Fleece award. Nonetheless, as more and more test failures occurred, the analysts were surprisingly successful in demonstrating that the reliability which would actually be experienced in the field some years hence would be a near-perfect 1.0. Their method for accomplishing this was simply to list each failure which had been encountered in the past and indicate the redesign which had been incorporated to preclude its recurring; ergo convincingly proving that future failures were impossible. Ironically, at the same time that this logic was gaining wide acceptance another major effort was getting underway to write the large number of instruction books which would be needed to explain how to repair the system when it was broken. This latter effort soon grew at such a pace that it became necessary to substantially increase its manning by shifting large numbers of engineers off of the effort which had up until then been devoted to redesigning the hardware to reduce failures.

A great deal of ink in advertising brochures is devoted to extolling the simplicity of operation and ease of maintenance of new products, both military and civilian. In cases where high complexity is incorporated into the item, the canonical reassurance given to purchasers is that all the complexity is "user transparent". . . supposedly meaning that the user doesn't need to be very smart to operate or fix the item in question. The fact is, however, that everyday twentieth-century life, in stark contrast with that of citizens existing a mere century earlier, is rife with encounters with broken hardware which its user has no idea whatsoever how to fix. How many homeowners, for example, can pull out their tool kit and repair a radar oven, an automobile's digital fuel controller, the synchronization on a color television, or even an electric toothbrush? Children's toys, generally presumed particularly susceptible to damage, require for their repair a working knowledge of microcircuitry as used in video-games, speech synthesizers, laser shooting galleries, fibre optic table decorations, and liquid crystal watch displays.

But if this is the situation for items merely intended for household use, what of high technology, state-of-the-art-challenging items designed to fly at Mach two, travel through space, or swim deep under the ocean? Or for that matter, what even of that earth-hugging machine to end all other machines, the tank?

The solution apparently in vogue to the above-mentioned difficulty has been observed by Lt. General Paul Gorman: namely, to provide ever more detailed instructions for the use and repair of each successive generation of new hardware. Consider as but one example the page count of technical manuals provided with the following tanks:

TANK	YEAR	NUMBER OF PAGES IN TECHNICAL MANUAL
M-26	1940	8,000
M-47	1950	9,000
M-48	1960	12,000
M-60	1970	15,000
M-60A3	1975	23,000
M-1	1980	40,000

The trend indicated in the above table, which can be shown to have rather general applicability, provokes a number of awkward conclusions. For example, another trend has already been observed toward increasingly complex equipment and a concomitantly shorter mean time between failures. Thus the situation will eventually be reached wherein everything is breaking more rapidly than the instruction books on how to repair them can be read. . . or possibly even written.

The solution might at first appear to be simply to develop more reliable and more easily used equipment; but this has already been shown to be altogether impossible. The real solution, the more straightforward one, is to place greater demands on the intelligence and ability of the operators and maintainers—in short, to develop a breed of superhuman humans.

Unfortunately, it is one more testimonial to the fact nature is not simply indifferent but is actually belligerent that at the very moment such increased capabilities are most needed the intelligence of humans is beginning to decline. This is verified in Figure 45 which illustrates that, although the information which must be absorbed in order to use space-age machinery is increasing markedly, the in-

The Rise and Fall of Human Knowledge

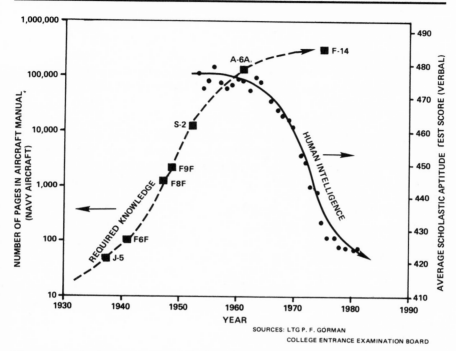

Figure 45   *At the same time that the information which is required to use and maintain modern hardware is increasing dramatically, the ability to comprehend that information is decreasing symmetrically.*

telligence of the humans who must use it is, as measured by that infallible standard, College Board scores, actually decreasing.* We thus have a situation where man has been progressively evolving upward from the ape for nearly *14 million years* and just at the very moment when his utmost intelligence is needed, at the dawn of the space-age, what should happen but his intelligence peaks out in 1956 and begins the long process of devolution back to the ape.

It seems that those individuals who have long been proclaiming that we should conduct a search for intelligent life in the solar system may *not* have been guilty of an oversight.

As the beleaguered director of engineering for the new Washington, D. C. Metro subway system explained to a *Washington Star* reporter when it was belatedly discovered that the weight of passengers in a car

---

*The author is indebted to Lt. General Paul F. Gorman for pointing out this connection.

caused its structure to flex such that the doors jammed, "We'd have great cars if it weren't for the passengers."

Once again, what a time for the roof to leak. Just when it is raining.

But *still another* problem yet remains to be confronted: Law Number IX stated that hardware will soon cost so much that none will be affordable. How can this square with the evidence just shown in Figure 45? The answer lies in the Law of Mind Over Matter (If no one minds then it doesn't matter):

If current trends prevail, hardware will be too costly to manufacture or purchase;but there will be a thriving market in the sale of instruction books on how to use it.

(LAW NUMBER XXXV)

The situation is aptly summarized by the apocryphal story of the gentleman who, lacking any cheese, baited his mousetrap with a *picture* of some cheese. To his acute disappointment, he is said to have caught a picture of a mouse. Thus, when no one can any longer afford to purchase hardware (giving due recognition to the fact that the equipment of the future would in actuality be of extremely high capability and sophistication were in fact anyone able to afford any of it), the thriving trade of the time will be the sale of *instruction manuals* . . .albeit for nonexistent products. A best seller list at that time might contain such provocative titles as "Do-It-Yourself Repair of Your Imaginary Rolls Royce," "How to Fix Your Model T-422A Light Emitting Diode," "Bubble Memory Repair Made Easy," "Self Diagnosis for Your New Automatic Test Equipment," or "Self-Taught Robot Repair."

But the most discouraging piece of evidence is the now well-established decline in human intelligence. Modest extrapolation of the data in Figure 45 reveals that, if the trend of the late 1960's and 1970's prevails, in just 142 years there will be no perceptible intelligence left whatsoever. Widespread discussion takes place even today about the need to write maintenance manuals at the level of a sixth-grade reader. This desire for simplicity of instruction, reaching its zenith in the case of children's products, is presumably why the instructions provided for one well-known electric train set are replete with passages such as the following: "The reversing switch changes the polarity of the main line. The polarity on either side of the upper insulated rail joiners now agrees so the locomotive can move off the reversing loop section and back onto the main. Note that the loop direction switch was never thrown, only the reversing switch. The loop direction switch is thrown when a train is on the reversing loop only when it is desired to make that train back up. Obviously if it was desired to run around the reversing loop clockwise, the loop direction switch and the track switch would be set opposite to the position shown (in the figure) before the train approaches the reversing loop."

Or why the assembly instructions for a widely marketed doll house direct: "Insert friction spring in right groove of bottom sash and hold with forefinger; insert spring in left hand groove and hold with thumb. Tip sash and place into frame removing forefinger slowly and push spring against right side joint. . . Place header in corner of jig, smooth side down. . . Assemble mitered casing in jig as shown and apply to inner frame using sill and apron."

Kid stuff!

Nonetheless, one suspects that the day must be near at hand when the bottom two ranks in the military will no longer be Private and PFC, but instead will have to be Private and PhD.

Murphy knew this all along. "When all else fails," he counseled, "read the instructions."

So Old for Its Age

*The first Indian hospital was built
in the U.S. last year. It took 400 years
from the time the white man arrived here.
Just think what the Indian must have to look
forward to in the next 400 years.*

Will Rogers

*At the retirement party for the chief engineer there was
much reminiscing about his early days on the project shortly
after he had graduated from college. It was pointed out how
his career had skyrocketed him through the organization;
first as a designer during the initial proposal phase, then as a
task leader during the engineering design phase, subsequently as a group engineer for the first redesign, as
section chief on the second, and finally as chief engineer
where he made his mark doing failure analyses during the
crashes. Here, truly, was a man who proved the invalidity
of the Peter Principle, rising not one but several levels
above his level of competence.*

The following law, dealing with program geriatrics, explains how
World War II was won in about half the time it takes today to develop
a new military system.

Figure 46 shows that the average major system development for
national defense now takes slightly over eight years to complete.
Interestingly, the *doing* time (for example, the time from the beginning
of the design of a new airplane until its first flight) has not changed
significantly during the last quarter of a century, as can be seen in
Figure 47. Apparently nostalgia just isn't what it used to be.

What *has* changed is the decision/approval time it takes to get a
new program started, together with the time it takes to get the end
product fielded once the development has been completed. The
historical ratio of *planning* time to *doing* time for a number of major
system developments is shown in Figure 48. On the average, the total
time it takes to develop a new system, including decision and approval time, has been increasing at a rate of 3 months per year, for 15
years. This has culminated in the recommendation that progress no
longer be measured in terms of milestones. Inchstones are said to be
more appropriate.

189

Duration of Development Programs

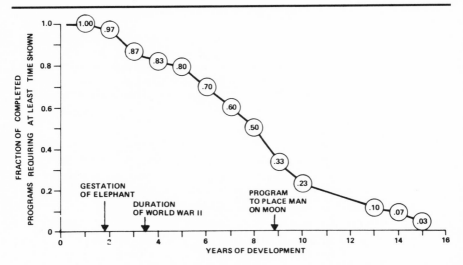

Figure 46   The median Engineering Development program conducted in the last two decades has stretched over eight years from start of full development to initial operational fielding. Seventeen percent of the programs have, however, managed to be completed in less than four years, providing at least an existence theorem for more rapid transition from the laboratory to the field.

Trends in Development Time

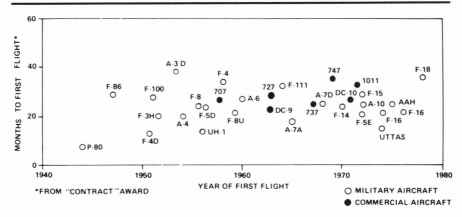

Figure 47   The duration of the design and build phase of development programs has remained virtually unchanged for forty years. In the case of aircraft, this period is approximately the same for government projects, commercial projects and, for that matter, projects undertaken in the Soviet Union.

Relationship of "Decision" Time to "Doing" Time

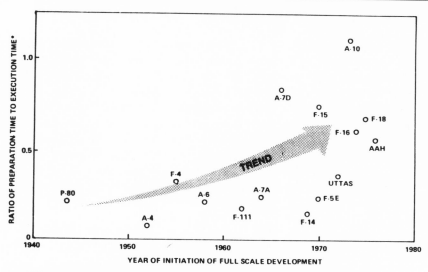

Figure 48   The time which elapses from agreement upon a need for a new item to the start of a program to fulfill that need has steadily increased, as has the time from first flight of a development article to deployment of a substantive operational capability. These are the principal contributors to schedule longevity.

Dr. Gene Fubini, a former Chairman of the Defense Science Board and one-time Assistant Secretary of Defense, describes an incident during World War II wherein he proposed a new electronic countermeasures technique to the Navy. Asked how quickly he could produce the item, he promised, "Just as quickly as you can make up your mind that you want it." The Captain responsible for electronic warfare devices, apparently a pragmatist, responded knowingly, "If it takes that long then I don't want it."

The Captain, if he could see the management system as it exists four decades later, would probably apply for preventive sick leave.

Based in part on the fact that the half-life of most technologies has been determined elsewhere to be on the order of ten years (far less in the case of electronics), it appears that if current glacial developmental trends persist, most new systems will be obsolete only slightly before they are born. This leads to the Law of Extended Gestation (also known as the Law of Deferred Gratification):

Never commit to complete a project within six months of the end of the fiscal year. . .in either direction.

(LAW NUMBER XXXVI)

The current record for prolonged gestation is jointly held by the Patriot and Aegis air defense radar systems, either of which eclipses the proverbial elephant by some 15 years. Each was one of those instant successes that took eighteen years. It is readily understandable, then, that there is not inconsiderable concern that those planning and budgeting for these programs may learn of studies by biologists that attribute the incredible success of a bat's "radar" (including chirp pulse compression) to over 50 million years of continuing perfection. All we need is a little more time.

If American aerospace products reflected the process that produces them, we would be the only nation in the world whose aircraft take bird strikes from behind.

Meetings Dismissed

*This is the saddest story
I have ever heard.*

F. M. Ford, 1915

*It was the first anniversary of starting testing for the third
time and the program was now under open attack from its
foes. Management's seemingly brilliant stroke of launching
an intensive advertising campaign when first inundated with
technical problems appeared to have failed abysmally.
Somehow problems persisted in spite of this enlightened
management tactic. Many of the program's foes now
proudly proclaimed that they had opposed the project back
in the days before it was even known what it would
comprise. The time expended in preparing all the
exhaustive reports these detractors now demanded to
explain why the program was slipping behind schedule —
just a part of the never ending chore of repelling boarders
— was beginning to take its toll on the project's participants.
In addition, the government program manager was under
investigation by OSI, FBI, GAO and KGB for having accepted a necktie from a contractor. Responding to this
situation, the customer and the contractor acquiesced to the
critics' demands that daily status meetings be held wherein
the workforce would be afforded the opportunity to stand
before an assembled throng and report at length the
reasons behind the lack of progress the previous day. In
addition, separate meetings would be scheduled to review
budgets, planning, and personnel assignments ...also on a
daily basis. Finally, a Master Meeting was established for
each morning during which the scheduling of all other
meetings would be coordinated, and a cost-control meeting
was scheduled for each evening to discuss how overtime
could be reduced. Thus would be solved the problem which
had become uncomfortably evident: everyone was working
so hard that no one had time to do any work.*

Herm Staudt, during his service as Undersecretary of the Army,
observed at the outset of an arduous thicket of briefings, "I always

come to these meetings with a problem. I always leave with a briefing and a problem."

The first fifty-six minutes of a meeting (*all* meetings require one hour) are, in fact, relatively innocuous and pass with little being accomplished other than the presentation of routine and generally peripheral background material. In the remaining four minutes, however, The Bombshell will invariably be dropped squarely on the center of the table. Thusly: the first fifty-six minutes will be devoted to heated debate among all participants as to the color the prototype aircraft should be painted for its forthcoming media debut. Only during the final four minutes will it gradually begin to emerge that just that morning the lone prototype crashed.

At The Bombshell, the harried decisionmaker, already late for the initial fifty-six minutes of the next meeting, is presented with three options. Based upon the anatomy of Pentagon decision-making, we know the first of these options will, unfortunately, require absolute surrender. The third, on the other hand, will demand funding of slightly over one gross national product (per year). The middle option, then, will offer a course that has as its sole redeeming virtue that it is the choice the staff wants you to select!

In the late 1960's, an Admiral contacted the Deputy Director of Defense Research and Engineering and strenuously objected to a decision paper that had been prepared for the Secretary of Defense — on the grounds that the paper contained only *two* options. Upon further discussion, it emerged that the Admiral's own preferred option was, in fact, one of the alternatives presented. The resulting enigma was resolved only when the exasperated flag officer blurted out in a moment of candor, "You *know* the Secretary always selects the middle option."

The "middle-option" approach presumably derives from the school of thought that you can fool some of the people all the time and all the people some of the time. . .and that's enough.

But meetings to discuss such programmatic matters as schedule problems should not be demeaned: recognition must be given to the fact that a great deal of effort is required even to *schedule* the schedule meetings. The first step in this process is for the chairperson to place a long-distance telephone call to the briefer to schedule the proposed briefing. This call will prove abortive because the briefer will always be at another briefing. The briefer later returns the chairperson's call only to learn that the chairperson is out of the office listening to a briefing. An average of 3.8 long-distance calls transpire (according to the author's actual sample) before contact is finally made. This process is known as Telephone Tag. Telephone Tag is not all bad; it helps make possible ATT's contribution to the tax base, and all the secretaries become very good friends.

Once a date is finally settled upon, the chairperson and briefer discover that the third requisite attendee cannot be available at the agreed-upon hour. The process then starts anew. The probability of finding a time when six people, each of whom already has a half-filled schedule, are simultaneously available is only about one in *thirty-two tries*. It can thus be demonstrated that meetings with more than ten busy people are mathematically impossible. The fact that many meetings take place with *more* than ten individuals present is not, it will be recognized, necessarily inconsistent with the above ob-servation.

It should be noted that the U. S. possesses a major strategic ad-vantage over the Soviet Union in the field of meeting-scheduling. This stems from the fact that one of the major impediments to telephonically coordinating meetings is the three-hour time difference between the east and west coasts of the U.S; it effectively reduces the available telephone-day to about five hours. The Soviet Union, faced with not just four but eleven different time zones, is virtually precluded from scheduling meetings with attendees from throughout the land. Many of these disappointed individuals are thus left with no alternative but to remain home and work.

In spite of these impediments, meetings, symposia, conventions, and fora flourish. Among the most popular of these events are gatherings far from one's place of work, since, as everyone recognizes, there are so many distractions where one works that no one can get any work done there. Figure 49 presents evidence collected over two centuries of the trend toward even more meetings. This explosion of meetings in distant parts of the world simply reflects the growing need to hold events on neutral turf, so as not to unduly inconvenience anyone. In this manner *everyone* can be in-convenienced.

Once a meeting finally takes place (it must necessarily be rescheduled yet another time because one of the principal attendees revises his vacation plans), protocol requires that the senior dignitary present be seated in the position of honor:at the head of the table — directly behind the large elevated reflector affixed to the viewgraph projector that permanently resides on the center of the table. This reflector effectively blocks from the decision-maker's view some forty-two percent of the projection screen, including that portion in the immediate center. This inevitable geometry very likely accounts for the reason senior officials always select the middle option:the first and the last ones are too dreadful to contemplate and the middle one can't be seen.

Meeting Obligations

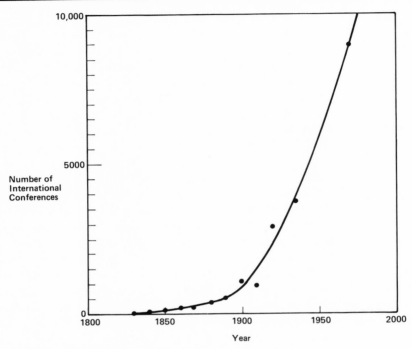

Source: John McHale, "World Facts and Trends"

Figure 49   The social acceptability of holding meetings as a mechanism for consuming management's time is expanding on all fronts. This is particularly true of international meetings, which bear the additional burden of absorbing large amounts of travel time.

In spite of such systemic limits passively accepted by most decision-makers, once an Air Force general with the Tactical Air Command actually had the audacity to take *control* of the meetings conducted for his benefit. Displaying ultimate disregard for the Code of the Briefer ("Power lies in the possession of the chalk"), he had the signal button for changing the viewgraphs placed *not at the podium but at his own seat!* Briefings thus took on an altogether new excitement and pace, with the last four minutes — people actually listened to them — sometimes lasting a full hour. This also provided fodder for a new form of wagering among the staff — on handicapping briefers.

But as has been noted, virtually all meetings are scheduled to consume exactly one hour (or, at the very "least," integral factors of one hour). Further, in accordance with Parkinson's Law, meetings never end early. In fact, as incredible as it may sound, there seems to be no such thing as a fifty-five-minute issue or a twenty-minute issue. All demand exactly one hour. Thus, during an eight-hour day it is possible to contend with only eight basic decisions, independent of whether the issues at hand relate to survival or to trivia.

One might assume that this optimal meeting interval is the consequence of years of evolutionary refinement, or at least is based on intensive studies by efficiency experts, decision theorists, and human-factors analysts. It is particularly regrettable, therefore, that one must observe that the duration of meetings has nothing whatsoever to do with the content of the material at hand, but rather is a consequence of the speed with which the Earth rotates about its axis (and, of course, the arbitary decision to divide this interval into twenty-four equal segments). If, for example, the Earth would rotate not in twenty-four but in eighteen hours, meetings would *almost certainly* be scheduled to occupy the resultant "new hour," now forty-five "minutes." A thirty-three percent increase in management productivity would thus be automatically realized, assuming the basic real workday remained unchanged. Not only does this suggest the excitement of an engineering undertaking that would dwarf the Apollo Moon project — it would use millions of rockets fastened around the Earth's equator, but also it would extend everyone's life expectancy (in days) by one-third.

Thus is derived Law of Meeting Objections, recognizing that managers tend to move throughout their realms whereas workers are more nearly fixed to their tasks:

If the Earth could be made to rotate twice as fast, managers would get twice as much done. If the Earth could be made to rotate twenty times as fast, all the managers would fly off and everyone else would get twice as much done.

(LAW NUMBER XXXVII)

The above law, it will be observed, is in contradistinction to the well-known Broadway show, "Stop the World; I Want To Get Off."

Some organizations, of course, do little *other* than hold meetings. This suggests that the absolute utility of meetings as a business artifice could perhaps somehow be deduced from an examination of the output of these particular institutions. . . which count among their numbers the Senate, the House of Representatives, and the United Nations. On the other hand, such an examination may not be a particularly good idea.

The fundamental fallacy of the ubiquitous meeting is epitomized in the observation of the chairman of the Board of Directors of SpaceTran Corp., Bill Sword, who reminds us that meetings last hours. . .but are documented in minutes.

On Doing Less with More

You can do almost anything with a bayonet. . .
except sit on it.
Napoleon

The lack of loyalty was astonishing to those who had devoted their careers to the project. That the very people for whom the product was intended would indicate at this late date that they didn't believe they needed the item came as a terrible blow. This negative attitude was widely attributed to the fact that there was no one left in the "user" community who had been around when the project started and had thus read the fine initial proposals. Worse yet, no copies of the original proposals were even available anymore, the files having been purged some years previously at the suggestion of the contractor's legal department to make room for failure analysis records. If only those early proposals were available it would, some believed, still be possible to build that proverbial silk purse. There is, in fact, a law which describes how one can make a silk purse out of a sow's ear. If, that is, one starts with a silk sow.

Although some types of systems are admittedly expensive, they clearly are also much more effective. Or are they? One such comparison can be made by examining the combat effectiveness of two classes of military systems having widely differing costs—guided missiles and guns. Figure 50 plots the military contribution of these two categories of systems during various major conflicts that have taken place since the advent of the missile age. In each of the conflicts considered, both types of systems were used fairly extensively, thereby providing a reasonably large data base. The combat impact of each category of system is measured in terms of the fraction of a given type of enemy materiel destroyed (airplanes, tanks, etc.) by missiles or guns, respectively. For example, the top-right "square" symbol would indicate that in some particular war in which both missiles and guns were employed, 96% of the targets of a particular class (say aircraft) were destroyed by projectiles costing about $90 each. (Actual labels have been omitted for security reasons.) The cost of the missile and gun systems is measured only in terms of "expendables," which is, of

Impact of Various Systems in Combat

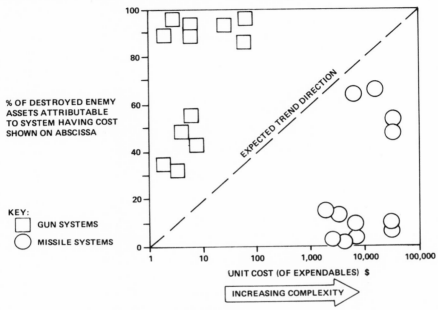

Figure 50 *Actual combat data from several wars indicate that the systems which had the greatest impact on the enemy were often those which were least costly and least complex. Care must, of course, be taken in generalization of this observation since low cost and low complexity are not necessarily synonymous with low technology.*

course, an oversimplification, but which is at least partially justified on the basis that the launchers (aircraft, ships, or the gun tube itself) are in fact reusable.

It might be presumed that the data points in such a comparison would aggregate along the dotted line shown in Figure 50; i.e., the more one pays for a system, the more it contributes. Disappointingly, the actual data points do not behave according to such a trend at all. Instead, they cluster into two distinct groups as far from the expected line as possible. The data points representing missiles indicate that, at least to date, such systems have had relatively less impact on the outcome of even modern battles than have the far less costly gun systems. This is presumably due in part to the increased susceptibility to countermeasures of the more sophisticated systems; but, more to the point, it is probably due to the fact that as equipment grows more costly, it can be afforded in far lesser quantities, thereby *sometimes* offsetting the hoped-for improvement in individual-item performance.

In these cases we seem to have spared no expense to assure there is no value.

Borrowing the words of a well-known congressman of some years ago, we seem to be even worse off than those he accused of knowing the price of everything and the value of nothing.

On the other hand, whoever heard of a military officer who got promoted for commanding a mine?

The next law, the Law of Inverse Contributions, derived with a good deal of liberty from empirical evidence, can be stated:

It is true that complex systems may be expensive, but it must be remembered that they don't contribute much.

LAW NUMBER XXXVIII)

The distinction between complex systems and high-technology systems is, in this regard, a crucial one. As technology matures there is reason to believe the above trend *could* in fact be reversed. But any failure to apply new technology in its least complex form is likely to produce, justifiably, still another generation of critics who want to push the lanyard.

Going Nowhere,
but Making Good Time

It is so soon that I am done for,
I wonder what I was begun for.

Tombstone
Cheltenham Churchyard

The telegram arrived at 3:00 p.m. on a Friday, just after the
stock market had closed. Ironically, most of the program
staff was away at the happy-hour which followed the
awards luncheon. It turned out to be the very day that the
marketing and legal departments were being honored for
their contributions to the program. That things were serious
became apparent when the announcement was made for
the entire legal department to return to the plant. No
mention was made of the engineers or factory employees.
The only common underpinning between the government's
and contractor's legal departments, an abiding concern that
peace might break out between the two respective
organizations' contracting groups, now seemed to be totally
dispelled. But somehow these events seem to portend ill,
substantiating the observation by a well-known college
football coach: "The light at the end of the tunnel may be a
freight train."

One consequence of the myriad of problems examined herein is a
relatively high mortality rate among development programs. This is a
condition which, incidentally, is rarely reflected in a contractor's long-
range sales plan, but which nonetheless is highly predictable in the
aggregate. Ill-conceived programs simply have highly foreseeable
outcomes; much as was suggested by another footballer, Sammy
Baugh, who answered a question as to whether the outcome of his
team's 73-0 defeat in the 1940 professional championship game
might not have been different had he scored first, by saying, "Sure. It
would have been 73 to 6."

The data presented in Figure 51 are derived from over 300
defense-related programs conducted in the past two decades and
verify the precariousness of most programs. They reveal the
probability that any given program will fail to survive the threats to its
existence which arise prior to any given year in its life. It is seen that

Survival Expectancy of Development Programs

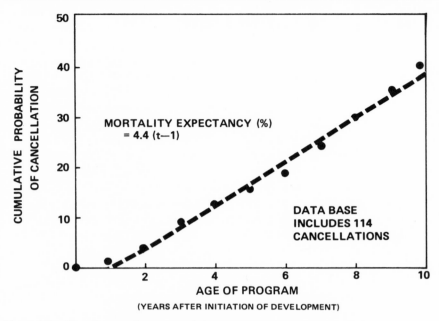

Figure 51   The chance of a program's being cancelled is more or less proportional to its exposure duration. Within limits, both cost and likelihood of cancellation are minimized by fully funding programs so that they can be conducted on a relatively aggressive schedule.

there is about a 4 percent probability of cancellation of a program each and every year except for the first year, sometimes referred to as the honeymoon period. Defeat can be snatched from the jaws of victory at almost any time. This appears to be relatively independent of program age, presumably even for such aged endeavors as the two aforementioned programs, which have successfully defied the laws of probability and soon will have been in development for 18 years. And it has been wisely observed that spending money on the design of military equipment to be put on the shelf is a darn good way to get your shelf captured.

Most projects in the acquisition arena seem to share the malady once attributed by Yogi Berra to an altogether different arena. "In Yankee Stadium," he explained," it gets late early."

The French poet and philosopher Paul Valery once noted, "The trouble with our times is that the future is not what it used to be." This seems to have quite literally been the case for the Condor missile program which has as its final entry in the System Acquisition Report to the Congress under the "Program Highlights" section the statement, "Program terminated by the Congress." Indeed many programs seem to have had a brilliant future behind them, as is recognized in the Law of Incomplete:

Most programs start out slowly and then sort of taper off.
(LAW NUMBER XXXIX)

In the above context, R&D is a four-letter word whose managers understand the chagrin of Iowa citizens who recently read in the weather forecast of their local paper that "there is a 90% chance of tomorrow."

This is of course a particularly disappointing conclusion in that nearly all new projects *begin* with such great promise and fanfare. But then, retired Lieutenant General and former astronaut Tom Stafford reminds us, "Yesterday's headlines are today's fish wrappers."

The existence of this law does provide encouragement, on the other hand, that not *all* managers are successful in working their programs into that position, apparently ultimately sought, wherein their termination costs exceed their cost-to-completion.

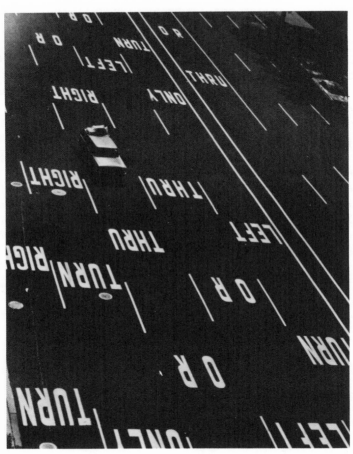

Courtesy of *Life Magazine*.

Chapter 6

Disaster Revisited

Watching the Watchers Watch

You may fire when you are ready, Gridley.
Admiral George Dewey
May 1, 1898

"This is probably the most important undertaking relating to your entire project," the speaker began at the staff meeting the morning following the demise. It was soon learned that this individual had been assigned to exhume the remains of the project and determine what had gone wrong so that it would never, ever, happen again. The speaker was obviously well qualified, having never had his professional reputation besmirched with the type of problems that had plagued the program whose entrails he was to examine. There were, of course, those few malcontents in the back of the room who mumbled something about the speaker having never been involved in any project, but even they were soon silenced by the enthusiasm of the undertaking, especially when the bus from headquarters arrived. The two least credible sentences in the English lanaguage have been said to be, "The check is in the mail" and "I'm from headquarters and I'm here to help you." As one beleaguered military installation newspaper inadvertently headlined, "Inspector General and Other Problems Arrive." Nonetheless, the effort to pin down blame began to gain momentum, eased enormously by the fact that several formerly key members of the project were no longer present. All in all, judging by the actions of both the auditors and the media, the program appeared to be in danger of becoming America's favorite spectator sport.

No doubt Inspectors General and other forms of overseers perform an extremely important role, but that role can be beneficial only when applied constructively and with considerable moderation. The prevailing trend would suggest the existence of an explosion in the overseer business, with an ominous threat approaching that there will soon be no one left for the auditors to audit. When this day of an infinite watcher-to-worker ratio arrives, it will presumably be necessary to focus audits on the mistakes which would have been made had in fact there been anyone doing anything. As Figure 52 indicates, the

The Auditing Boom

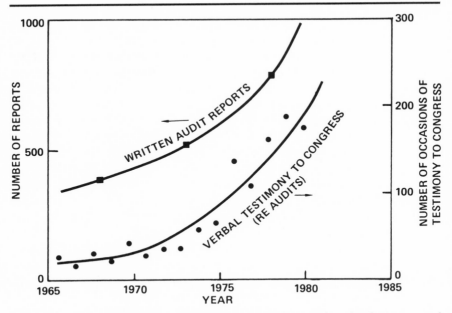

Figure 52   The amount of activity devoted to reviews and audits has increased markedly in recent years in spite of frequent protestations to the contrary.

increase in magnitude of the federal oversight effort is on the order of 200 percent per decade, possibly making it America's fastest growing industry. But perhaps this is to be expected in a world which pays a network television anchorman several times as much to *report* the news as it pays the President of the United States to *make* the news!

There are fully tens of thousands of federal auditors of one type or another at large today, of whom a disproportionately large 18,000* are assigned to ferret out the Department of Defense's transgressions. . .via both internal and external audits. No matter whether the production rate in the factory is one per month or 1000 per month, the grandstand is always full. Chuck Mills, a former football coach at Wake Forest, reminds us that a spectator is a person "who sits 40 rows up in the stands and wonders why a 17-year-old kid can't hit another 17-year-old kid with a ball from 40 years away. . .then he goes out to the parking lot and can't find his car."

---

*This total, it must be reported, is up from the 14,000 shown in the previous edition of this book.

One thing is certain: if you try to please everybody, somebody isn't going to like it.

A new branch of specialization is now emerging in order to assure that the auditors are themselves performing their assignments effectively; this new branch is called watching the watchers. The opportunities for still further expansion of this specialty are boundless. The creation of such specialties represents a breakthrough in that it insures the perpetuation of the trade even in the dread event that the last individual actually doing any work gets fed up with reviewers continually coming through the sidelobes and decides to join the legions of watchers overseeing his meager output. The media will perhaps note in passing this event by reporting something like: "The nation's work force, wearing a yellow shirt, today retired from active employment amidst a crescendo of criticism by the auditing community that the action was ill-conceived, mal-timed and mandatory of investigation."

In an effort to augment its number by recruiting amateur or part-time watchers, the Office of Management and Budget, an arm of the Administration, recently established a telephone hot-line to receive tips on waste in government. As luck would have it, the General Accounting Office, an arm of the Congress, had been planning to do exactly the same thing but was beaten to the switchboard by two days. The ensuing squabble over turf rights led *The Washington Star* to note editorially, "That raises the question of whether there is sufficient coordination or possibly a wasteful duplication of effort in the war on waste."

The process of proposal evaluation serves as an example wherein truly enormous numbers of manhours are expended, not so much to assist the decisionmaker in making good decisions but rather to build a protest-proof audit trail. Were the number of manhours involved in proposal evaluation cut by a factor of five, it is doubtful that the sources ultimately selected would differ substantially. . . but the ability to fend-off protests and audits might deteriorate markedly. The value of a Pearl Harbor file thus remains unchallenged.

The process of reviewing Determination and Findings (D&F's) is a case in point. One spot check several years ago revealed an average of 23 signatures and initials on this document which is required prior to the award of a negotiated contract. . . culminating, by law, in the signature of a Presidential appointee. Although several months are generally required for the processing of such documents, their principal value seems to reside purely in the theory of safety in numbers. As was commonly accepted advice in the early days of railroads in the Western United States, "Head for the roundhouse, boys; they can't corner us there."

Any bureaucrat worthy of the name will in fact soon strategize that a fail-safe way to guard against criticism is *never* to take risks, even when those risks may be very prudent and may have significant probable payoff. Extrapolating the theory that the only people who never make bad decisions are those who never make decisions, it can be logically concluded that the only people whose work cannot be criticized are those who produce no work. Managers thus quickly learn to fear bad news with even greater fervor than they covet good news. We are thereby inevitably led to the observation by Meg Greenfield of *The Washington Post* that "there is a profound commitment in this country today to not letting anything happen."

Or, as Bum Phillips, coach of the New Orleans Saints (and, as previously noted, former coach of the Houston Oilers), stated with equal profundity but perhaps less eloquence, "You gotta have rules, but you also gotta allow for a fella to mess up once in a while."

As the old saying goes, "There is a difference between giving and handing people their head."

All of which leads to the Law of Perpetual Emotion, borrowed from naval lore and based in turn upon the observation that reviewers seldom acquire ulcers. . .although many are suspected carriers:

Two-thirds of the Earth's surface is covered with water; the other third with auditors from headquarters.

(LAW NUMBER XL)

Murphy taught that if anything can go wrong it will, but it was left to Evans and Bjorn to point out that "no matter what goes wrong, there will always be somebody who knew it would." The only thing most audits fix is the blame.

But one contractor actually stumbled across the ultimate solution to the problem of a penetrating and intransigent plant auditor who had been assigned to oversee their activities: they wrote a letter to his supervisor praising the fine job he was doing!

Much Ado About Nothing

Speak with words that are soft and sweet.
You never know which ones you may eat.
American Cowboy Saying

Having completed the task of segregating the heroes from the villains, the effort turned to explaining to those fortunate enough to have not been involved in the project what had actually happened. It turned out that once again there was a great deal of historical precedence for even this sort of undertaking.

Major James Wesley Powell, organizer and leader of the first expedition through the rapids of the Grand Canyon, was basically a scientist. His major focus during the trip was on gathering technical data using such devices as his barometer, sextant, and keen powers of observation. His report on the trip, not surprisingly, was comprised almost entirely of detailed descriptions of the geological structure of the canyon. It must, therefore, have been to his great dismay a few years later, when the approval of funds he was seeking in his testimony before a congressional committee for further exploration was made conditional on his writing an *adventure* story on his earlier trip through the canyon!

Happily, this congressional insistence led to one of the truly great books on exploration. Unhappily, at least from Major Powell's viewpoint, it interfered with his getting on with the next phase of his research. Showing his usual resourcefulness, he did manage to limit the distraction by publishing a somewhat expanded version of his diary.

More modern adventurers through the treacherous rapids of the Congress have encountered not altogether dissimilar expectations, with demands being made on departmental officials for testimony with such frequency that many officials seemingly have little time to do anything but tell what they would have been doing if they had not been too busy testifying. In the author's own experience, due to a Machiavellian conjunction of confirmation hearings and the budget cycle, after having been on the job as a presidential appointee for only l-1/2 hours the next three *days* were spent providing testimony to the Congress. This distills down to about ten minutes in which to tell of each minute's work! In fairness, however, it must be pointed out that

213

214

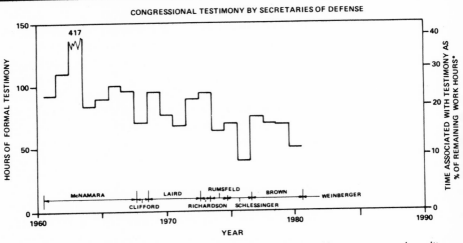

CONGRESSIONAL TESTIMONY BY SECRETARIES OF DEFENSE

Figure 53   Requirements for verbal and written reports, like reviews and audits, place heavy demands on the time of program participants and senior executives alike.

in the case of defense research and development hearings, the time spent justifying proposed expenditures is only about $2 million per minute.

Such problems are once again not unique to Capitol Hill. Every researcher has experienced the problem wherein so much time is spent in justifying his or her existence and in submitting periodic reports on work that was supposed to have been accomplished that little time remains during which to actually accomplish any work. A well-known American political figure suggested that had a company been formed some years ago to invent the electric light bulb using the present development process, that company would still be known today as "General Candle." Columbus and COMSAT would probably still be busy testifying on how they were going to get satellites to turn the corners as they passed around the edges of the earth.

The problem is that philosophizing is no substitute for *doing something* — doing something, as the saying goes, "even if it is right."

Once again, Yogi Berra has best captured the thought: "Ninety percent of this game," he said, "is half mental." The difficulty stems from the fact that some of the world's greatest discoveries have been made by accident by people not overly constrained in what they could pursue: x-rays, penicillin. . .and America, to name a few. Under such circumstances, many of the world's greatest forecasters might have been better suited for careers in silent radio.

But if words sometimes fall short of the mark, it certainly does not seem to have hurt the demand. Figure 53 presents information on the number of hours various Secretaries of Defense have devoted to delivering testimony before the Congress about what is to be done in the future or what was to have been done in the past. The figures shown do not, incidentally, include preparation time which, if assumed to equal three hours of preparation for each hour of testimony (a number which many veteran members of Congress would almost certainly view as highly suspect), brings the total time spent on testimony to about one-fourth of the time left for work. Encouragement might be derived from what appears to be a slight downward trend in verbosity, but earlier laws suggest this is merely a consequence of the increasing demands to spend time *writing* regulations. Not to mention providing *written* justification for budget requests which in the case of the FY84 budget, according to the Defense Department Comptroller, exceeded 21,000 pages.

A basic instability exists: if things go badly, then more and more time is consumed to explain what went wrong, thereby further decreasing the time available to manage, with the result that more and more things go wrong. On the other hand, if things go well, such as the Apollo program or the first Shuttle flight, it is difficult indeed for the key figures involved not to spend the next year or two responding to demands for speeches on how well things went.

The steady growth of the Congressional Record as a publishing enterprise bears eloquent witness to the validity of the Law of Oratorical Engineering (known in Roman times as Nero's Law):

The more time you spend talking about what you have been doing the less time you have to do anything. Eventually, you spend more and more time talking about less and less until finally you spend 100 percent of your time talking about nothing.

(LAW NUMBER XLI)

Growing Like a Regulation

The first thing we do,
let's kill all the lawyers.
Henry VI

Although a few of the workers on the defunct project elected to retire, most were soon well established in their new positions of greater responsibility in still another program which, happily, was just beginning at the time of the demise of the earlier ill-conceived undertaking. The experience gained over the years in dealing with such cantankerous problems proved to qualify most of them for substantial promotions. It had become, of course, agonizingly clear that the difficulties of the past could not be permitted to recur. In order to assure this, activity began with renewed intensity, particularly by those on the government side, to write regulations which would in fact prevent any such difficulties ever interfering with future projects. The senior managers concentrated on increasing the authority they reserved for themselves because the record of past mistakes clearly indicted that only the people at the very top could be relied upon.

The following law provides the mathematical foundation of Lamennais' apothegm, which states, "Centralization breeds apoplexy at the center and anemia at the extremities." The apparently inherent tendency of senior managers to draw unto themselves authority for making even minute decisions is nowhere more evident than in government, with the acquisition process being but one case in point. At each point along the way to the senior manager a pyramid of approval steps must be climbed, each inhabited by individuals often vested only with the authority for saying "no". . . and sometimes little accountability even for that. Thomas Carlyle referred to this process as "the everlasting no."

The futility of such extreme centralization was first recognized a number of years ago when Jethro, father-in-law to Moses, observed that great confusion reigned as Moses led his people out of the land of the Pharaoh. Jethro remarked that Moses seemed be sitting alone. . . "while all the people stand about you from morning to evening" awaiting direction. Dr. Mort Feinberg, the industrial psychologist, points out that Jethro became the first management consultant in history when he advised Moses, as recorded in the book of Exodus, "What you are doing is not good. You and the people with you will wear yourselves out, for the thing is too heavy for you; you are not able to perform it alone."

Teddy Roosevelt experienced the same sort of problem, albeit to a different scale: "I can do either one of two things," he complained; "I can be president of this country, or I can control Alice. I cannot possibly do both."

Sadly, the first evolutionary step from such "in-person" centralization is that of ruling by decree or regulation. It is pointed out by advocates of the latter process that increased delegation increases the risk of occasional failures. The counter to this is that the present system seems to be eliminating the risk of occasional successes. It will be recalled that the Charge of the Light Brigade was ordered by an officer who was not at the scene and was not familiar with the territory.

Large organizations seem to be particularly susceptible to the notion that regulations can become a substitute for sound management judgment. Until recently, for example, the U.S. government had imposed a set of 23,000 words of specifications on those who would sell to it a simple mousetrap. The specification for chewing gum totals 15 pages and the specification for Worcestershire sauce is said to run 17 pages.

The *Armed Forces Journal* points out that in 1946 the U.S. Atlantic Fleet comprised 778 ships (that had won a war) and sailed under regulations contained in a 72-page pamphlet. In contrast, today's Atlantic Fleet may only have 297 ships but it is well equipped with regulations. . .308 pages of them.

In spite of the profusion of established rules, it is soon discovered that special cases and special problems still somehow occur, each requiring additional rules for its prevention. Caught up in this fervor of eliminating all problems by regulating against them, the terminal phase is represented by what is known as the "hammer" syndrome described by Abraham Maslow: to wit, "If the only tool you have is a hammer, you tend to see every problem as a nail."

But none of this matters anyway. Most builders of high-technology systems are sufficiently intransigent that they would view even the Ten Commandments as no more than the Ten Suggestions.

Of course, as new rules are added, none of the old rules are ever discarded; none, that is, until the entire management-by-regulation concept disintegrates of its own weight and a new cycle begins based on an altogether new set of regulations. But the whole approach

Growth of a Regulatory System

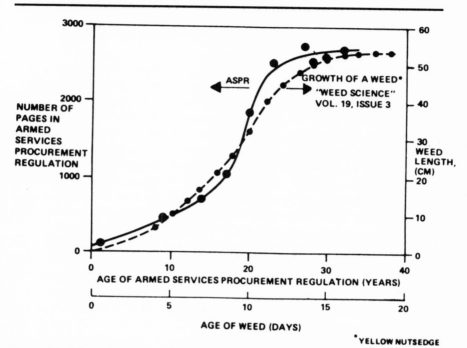

Figure 54 The volume of regulations imposed on participants in engineering and production activities has grown rapidly with time, paralleling the behavior of certain natural phenomena. The imposition of regulations can sometimes be quite subtle, for example flowing down references to subordinate regulations. In one such case, a court held a contractor liable for failure to comply with a regulation at the fifth level of an indentured tree of specifications cited only in references.

collapses because, as a veteran worker confided to a student (later to become a national union leader) beginning a summer's employment in a large factory, "if you *really* want to mess up the company, do exactly what they tell you."

One particularly interesting but unfortunately not atypical example of the growth of regulations is to be found in the Armed Services Procurement Regulation (ASPR) which has governed procurement of everything used in the nation's defense, from aircraft carriers to the paper on which the ASPR itself was printed. Figure 54 shows the rate of growth of ASPR over its lifetime and verifies that it indeed exhibits a behavior consistent with well-established growth processes observed in nature. It is also noted that, based solely on its growth pattern, the

ASPR appears to have reached its terminal phase—after which it can be expected to be replaced by a new set of policies* which, like their predecessors, will remain undaunted by the fact that the Ten Commandments themselves required only 99 words for their statement. Thus, it can be seen that, to borrow the proverbial expression, there is bad news and there is good news. The bad news is that our regulations don't work. The good news is that we've got lots of them.

Not only does the length of individual regulatory and policy documents increase with time, but so also does the number of such documents. For example, the number of policy documents listed in the umbrella defense acquisition policy statement (DOD 5000.1/.2) was 15 in 1971 and 26 in 77. But this hardly reflected the beginning: by 1980 there were 114 documents listed. Seemingly for every action there is an equal and opposite government policy. . . and when it come to areas which are as yet free of volumes of regulation, it can be said that it is not nature alone which abhors a vacuum.

The comment of Charles Schulz on the cover of Dr. Laurence Peter's renowned book, *The Peter Principle*, seems to apply with broad generality: "Great! This book will probably change my life. At least, I think it will. Maybe it won't."

With all these safeguards against problems, one would expect a veritable flood of reports of programs successfully completed within budget. One such report poured in a few years ago. But overall, it is clear that not much has been accomplished other than to tie the hands of those who in fact happen to be able managers.

Former Undersecretary of the Navy Jim Woolsey observes that before doing any work we will soon have to fill out Mission Element Need Statements, Environmental Impact Statements, Arms Control Impact Statements, and Impact Impact Statements. It may be that Japan graduates nearly twice as many engineers as the U.S. with less than half the latter's population and is devastating U.S. industry in the competitive marketplace, but Japan will have considerable difficulty matching the U.S. strength in the preparation of paperwork due to our lead of 20 to 1 in the number of lawyers per capita, not to mention 7 to 1 in accountants. Few if any nations can present a challenge to us in terms of the number of suers and suees in our litigious society.

Unfortunately this plethora of guidance has not been totally suc-

---

*ASPR has recently been superseded by the "DAR" (Defense Acquisition Regulation). This in turn has for a number of years been planned to become subsidiary to the "FAR" (Federal Acquisition Regulation), a term particularly descriptive of the timeframe in which it apparently will actually become available.

cessful in freeing those who are to be protected from at least a residual degree of uncertainty and confusion. Consider the "test of applicability" proposed in the recent Air Force directive on new approaches to materiel acquisition which instructs the reader to "select four but not less than two acquisitions on which to apply the test." Or the Federal Communications Commission application form which requires (original emphasis): "All fees have been suspended January 1, 1977. DO NOT SEND FEES UNTIL FURTHER NOTICE. MAILING APPLICATION: Mail your application and fee to the Federal Communications Commission, P.O. Box 1030, Gettysburg, Pa. 17325." Or the Air Force draft environmental impact statement for the MX missile which profoundly advises anxious readers that "Utah prairie dogs do not occur in Texas or New Mexico."

When in 1981 the President issued a half-page memorandum instructing federal agencies to cut back on "superfluous" publications, the Office of Management and Budget quickly released a ten-page "bulletin" explaining what he meant. Then they followed this with a twenty-page "control plan" explaining what *they* had meant. Presumably of particular value were the eight attachments and the new form provided to implement the instruction.

But the all-time classic is the following excerpt from an Equal Employment Opportunity Commission management directive: "REPORTING REQUIREMENTS: Federal agencies and designated major operating components (as described in MD-702) are required to submit their sexual harrassment plans to the Office of Government Employment EEOC, 60 days after effective date of this directive." The next step will presumably be a request for a listing of all employees broken down by sex.

Fortunately, problems caused by the lack of straightforward wording have not gone unrecognized and a new document has found its way through the system entitled "Air Force Program for Making Departmental Publications Understandable by Users." Among its solutions to the problem at hand: "It is proposed that directorate level OPR review and deletion of recertification of essentiality be accomplished on all Air Force publications." Clearly, problems of regulatory misunderstanding will soon be a thing of the past.

It is also a source of some consternation that for years the government has been issuing directives to industry regarding one of its favorite topics. . . saving money by standardization. . . on 8 x 10 paper—the use of which is unique in the free world to none other than. . . the U.S. Government!

But fortunately it has been possible for the U.S. paper industry to keep pace with this ever-increasing demand which can be shown to be very closely represented each year since 1900 by the equation: consumption of paper (pounds) $= 67e^{0.03(\text{Year}-1900)}$. Holding up its end of the bargain, the federal government in 1978 purchased the equivalent of over 66 *billion* sheets of paper.

The management school floundered on this principle appears to have adopted the lowly squid as its model: " When in trouble, cover it with ink."

The net impact of the weed-like growth of regulations has been eloquently stated by S. W. Tinsley of Union Carbide Company in response to criticism leveled a few years ago by government officials at U.S. industry for its failure to create new products which would provide the jobs to eliminate unemployment and generate the exports to reverse the adverse trade balance. Tinsley's reply: "Government officials keep asking us where are all the golden eggs, while the other part of their apparatus is beating the hell out of our goose!"

One recent Request for Proposal cited, *among others*, the following social and economic programs with which compliance was required: Buy American Act; Preference for United States Food, Clothing and Fibers; Clean Air Act of 1970; Equal Employment Opportunity Act; Anti-Kickback Act; Fair Labor Standards Act of 1938; Acquisition of Foreign Buses; Release of Product Information to Consumers; Prohibition of Price Differential; Required Source for Jewel Bearings; Gratuities; Prison-made Supplies; Care of Laboratory Animals; Required Source of Aluminum Ingot; Small Business Act; Labor Surplus Area Concerns; National Women's Business Enterprise Policy; Noise Control Act; Resource Conservation and Recovery Act of 1976; Federal Water Pollution Act; Officials Not to Benefit; Convict Labor Act... and others. Most assuredly, as another law points out, we have not left disaster to chance.

It is to be emphasized that many of these endeavors are probably extremely worthwhile. It is suggested only that this worth should be exposed to the sunshine, with the cost of complying with each provision being separately priced and not buried in the cost of achieving some other capability which is being sought. Only in this manner can cost-benefit judgments be soundly exercised.

Attempts have even been made to regulate warfare out of existence, such as the resolution introduced by Eldridge Geary at the Continental Congress in 1787. Geary's resolution to limit the size of the Continental Army, by law, to 10,000 was defeated only after George Washington was heard to mutter, in effect: "A very good idea. Let us also limit the size of any invading force to 5,000 men!" More recently, in 1982, it was left to the Supreme Court to rule that the U.S. Navy could continue its long-established bombing practice on the island of Vieques, even though the Navy had not been granted a pollution permit under the Federal Water Pollution Control Act.

We are thus led to the Law of Consternation of Energy:

The ubiquitous regulation, created as a management surrogate, takes on a life of its own and exhibits a growth pattern which closely parallels that of selected other living entities observed in nature; most specifically, weeds.

(LAW NUMBER XLII)

No fewer than 324,000 regulators are today employed by the Federal Government alone. . . a number equal to the combined populations of thirteen of the nation's state capitals. John Heywood noted nearly five centuries ago, "Ill weed groweth fast." John Heywood knew even more than he knew.

Regulatory Geriatrics

How long halt ye between two opinions?
I Kings 18:21

The effort to generate regulations proved to be a very satisfying one. There was, for example, no longer the continued aggravation of the people from the test lab incessantly pointing to still another failure. Further, the experience in writing the failure reports ironically proved to be excellent training for writing rules and policies, and there still remained a few individuals who could even reach all the way back to experience gained in writing the original proposal for the program. But as the words flowed and good times prevailed, some unspoken doubts began to arise, particularly among the old-timers, as to how effective the new rules would actually prove to be in legislating problems out of existence.

Abigail Adams once remarked, "We have too many high-sounding words, and too few actions that correspond with them." Law Number XLII informs us that we similarly have many high-sounding regulations, but among them precious few solutions to our problems. Each time we seek to solve a *problem*, we somehow seem to depart with a regulation and a problem. . .to paraphrase the earlier observation concerning meetings.

It was previously noted that regulations tend to grow like weeds. The truth is, however, that it would be fortunate indeed if regulations did grow like weeds. Weeds, it seems, are a member of the "annuals" family and, therefore, survive only for one year. Regulations, on the other hand, are seen in Figure 55 to endure an average of not one but seven years (at which time they are, of course, replaced by still another regulation. . . or two. . . or. . .). In fact, a quarter of the regulations created have a life expectancy exceeding ten years.

There is an element of cyclical behavior in regulatory pronouncements which is discernable as alternating generations of regulators, in their zeal to avoid emulating their *immediate* predecessors, repeat the errors of their forebearers once-removed. This is called the pendulum principle and is the cause of the phenomenon whereby people who have lived too long will recognize each "new" initiative which is introduced with appropriate fanfare as merely a reincarnation of some

Regulatory Geriatrics

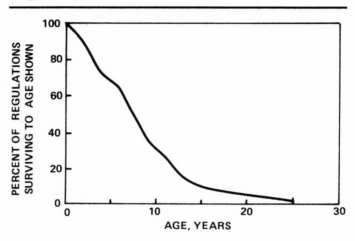

DATA SOURCE: DOD DIRECTIVES SYSTEM
QUARTERLY INDEX

Figure 55   Once created, most regulations have proven to be extremely durable before being eliminated or, more likely, being replaced with several new regulations. The attempt to use regulations as a surrogate for management competence does not appear to rank among mankind's greater successes.

earlier idea long ago discarded. We thus learn to commit old sins in new ways. But this does not dissuade each new generation of regulators from promulgating anew its rediscovered philosophies. Presumably it would be for the common good were the approach of Lloyd Smith, coach of the Toronto Maple Leafs, to be adopted: "I have nothing to say," he said," and I'm only going to say it once."

The average top-level government official (presidential appointee) has, over the past decade, demonstrated a survivability in his or her position of 2.1 years. Herein lies the root of the weed problem: one can achieve *bureaucratic immortality* by creating regulations which will endure long after their procreator has passed into oblivion. This proves to be an almost irresistible temptation.

But if the life expectancy of a regulation is so *long* as to inspire mortal policymakers to create them, it is much too *short* to provide the continuity needed to assure a stable lifetime for the average piece of hardware. Such hardware requires 8.3 years merely to develop and remains in the inventory for 23 years thereafter in the case of an airplane and 33 years in the case of a ship (even excluding the lag between the end of development and the production of any individual item). Thus, viewing the development phase alone, there is in that period an average of one complete turnover of the regulations which were in-being when a project was initiated, resulting in a whole superstructure of totally new regulations imposed subsequent to its birth. Compound this regulatory turbulence during these formative years with the 3 DSARC's (Defense Systems Acquisition Review Council decision-making meetings), 4 successive sets of senior officials, 8 budget cycles, and 144 votes in Congress on funding, and the miracle is not that many programs fail to survive but rather that some programs actually survive to fail!

The real hazard is that regulations sometimes endure long enough to take on altogether different meanings than were originally intended. The "Prompt Payment Act" offers a non-trivial example. The Congress, concerned over the siphoning from the defense industry of capital needed for investments, discovered that a few government paying centers were sometimes delinquent in meeting contractors' bills by two, three, and even more months (although the great majority were paying within a few weeks). To discipline the slow-disbursers, the Congress passed legislation, the "The Prompt Payment Act," demanding that all bills thereafter be paid within thirty days. Unfortunately, those who implemented the legislation issued instructions that all bills were to be paid *on the thirtieth day!* The net result was a further outflow of capital from the defense industry and a decrease in its ability to make capital investments. The "Prompt Payment Act" thus, as might be expected in a world where cutting red tape means splitting it lengthwise, actually *delayed* payment!

The law which has been found empirically to describe this proclivity of regulations to endure beyond the life of their creator (but pass away before their dependent systems) is sometimes referred to as the Law of Enduring Pestilence. It states:

The average regulation has a life span one-fifth as long as a chimpanzee and one-tenth as long as a human, but four times as long as the official who created it.

(LAW NUMBER XLIII)

Many of today's problems were yesterday's solutions.

Employer of Only Resort

Nobody goes there anymore
because it's too crowded.
Yogi Berra

If the top management of the contractor had by now arrived at the conclusion that it would have to maintain much greater personal control over future undertakings, this was even truer among the government managers. Furthermore, by bringing more tasks into the government for execution as well as direction, it would be possible to eliminate unnecessary costs which had been incurred previously in establishing competitive sources, evaluating proposals, and the like. Furthermore, there would be savings achievable by no longer having to pour money into unproductive areas such as profits. The aphorism which relates to these considerations corroborates the late Senator Everett Dirksen's observation about big government: "A billion here, and a billion there," he lamented, "and pretty soon it adds up to real money."

The percentage of civilian workers in the United States employed by government at the federal, state, and local levels is displayed in Figure 56. A growth trend is observed which has been very predictable and monotonic throughout the history of the nation. A modest extrapolation into the future, shown by the dotted portion of the trend line, indicates that the time is not too distant when one can expect 100 percent of the working population, and probably some who are not, to be employed by the government. Taking the next logical step, one can state the Law of Instinctive Herding:

By the time of the Nation's Tricentennial, there will be more government workers in the United States than there are workers.

(LAW NUMBER XLIV)

Thus will finally mark the replacement of the civil servant by, unfortunately, the civil serpent. Significantly, the Civil Service Commission, which was established to exercise control over the bureaucracy, has outstripped its dominion by growing at a rate five times that of the Federal Government as a whole.

Growth of Government

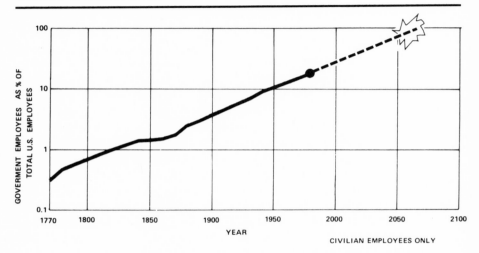

Figure 56   The fraction of the nation's workforce which is employed by government at all levels is on a steady course.

The Nation's Most Productive Industry

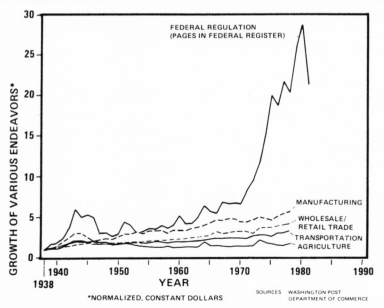

Figure 57   The growth of regulations has far outstripped the the growth of other less productive segments of the economy.

Some years ago the vulnerability of the federal work force was severely tested when on heavy snow-days in Washington, D.C., the policy was adopted of announcing over the radio that "only essential employees need report to work." Attendance on those days is a carefully guarded secret.

A nonnegligible by-product of the boom in government employment is, of course, the already-observed explosion of the regulation business. When capable individuals are placed in positions with no access to factories or other means of productive output, it is instinctive to devote themselves to the regulation of those who do. The suspicion that the productivity of Regulators has far outstripped the rate of increase of output of Regulatees is verified by the data shown in Figure 57. Perhaps the foremost index of productivity of Regulators is the number of pages in the *Federal Register*. . . sort of the *Literary Digest* of the regulation business, but with an interest level that rates it slightly ahead of the *Congressional Record* but still well behind the *Commerce Business Daily*.

One final step in the descent of productive growth, however, remains: for the government simply to take over the economy itself and establish a new order based totally on the production of regulations.

But this could never happen in a society founded on the principles of free enterprise.

For What It's Worth, Save Your Money

Every man's life, liberty and
property are in danger when the
Legislature is in session.
Daniel Webster

And so draws to a close the final chapter in the tortured life
of our program gone awry. It proved to have been sadly
correct that the motion picture telling the tale of this project
would have had a much happier ending had it been shown
backward. But such is the nature of high-technology un-
dertakings near the edge of the state-of-the-art. . . par-
ticularly when it is not altogether clear which side of the
edge they are on. Nonetheless, optimism continues at a
high level since all the participants in the earlier debacle are
now firmly entrenched in their new postions with the
government; ample funds are available; the nuisance of
competitors constantly yapping at their heels is gone; and,
best of all, they are now part of the fastest-growing team
anywhere in the technological community.

The trend in the growth of government as measured by the number of people it employs is, of course, paralleled by the government's financial receipts; and in turn by the government's ability to conduct its own programs on its own behalf as it sees fit. For example, there is now a tax collector somewhere in the U.S. extracting a dollar every 25 milliseconds—including roughly half of each dollar of the profits earned by industry. The average citizen now works until May 11 of each year simply to pay his or her taxes. By extrapolating the trend shown in Figure 58, it can be seen that the government will by the year 2120 have all the money that is generated in the U.S. economy and, as has already been noted, it will directly employ all the people about 60 years prior to that time. What will happen during the interim period between these dates is not yet clear, but poses the interesting question of whether the last person left in the private sector will have to support the entire nation's work force, or whether he or she instead will individually enjoy the full benefit of those residual funds not yet controlled by the government.

In terms of the fraction of the gross national product absorbed in government receipts, one can also use the extrapolation presented in

234

The Demise of Free Enterprise

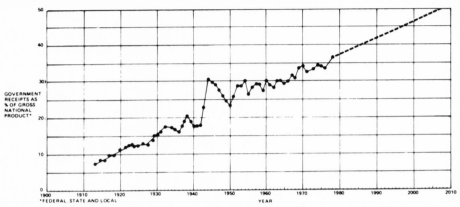

Figure 58 Governmental dominance of the national economy has followed a generally consistent trend for many years, with only minor setbacks following major wars. The U.S. lags the Soviet Union and China by only about 125 years, Sweden by 52 years, and England by still less. This trend should finally help establish the strong bond which some say is lacking in the U.S. between government and industry since even today government truly is industry's partner, thoughtfully sharing the fruits of industry's labors with industry on a roughly fifty-fifty basis (not including, of course, the government's subsequent additional sharing of any dividends that flow to the owners of industry).

Figure 58 to ascertain that the U.S. lags England by only 17 years and Sweden by only 56 years in this respect. As Senator S. I. Hayakawa has noted, regarding his experience in reviewing money legislation, "So in five minutes we have disposed of two *billion bucks*, two billion, not two million; I never realized it could be so easy. It's all simple addition. *You don't even have to know subtraction!*"

Bill Schneider, an Associate Director of the Office of Management and Budget in Washington, warns that "one thing we must particularly guard against is the danger that we might get all the government we pay for." President Reagan puts it in slightly different terms according to *RWR: The Official Ronald Wilson Reagan Quote Book*. . . to wit: "Government is like a baby—an alimentary canal with an appetite at one end and no sense of responsibility at the other."

The challenge which this unrelenting trend will pose for future presidents is stupefying. George Washington, for example, needed to dispose of only $14,031 per day during his period in office. Abraham Lincoln, abetted by a war, needed to sign checks for but $2,228,989 each day. Even Franklin Roosevelt had to contend with only $82,679,783 per day, but by Jimmy Carter's time his responsibilities for spending had grown to $1,318,298,426 daily. Think of the challenge found by whoever will be president in the year 2000 and, based on this trend, will awaken each morning faced with the task of unloading 5 trillion dollars before nightfall.

Of course, the possibility does remain that inflation may yet make this easy.

The significance of these observations to an industrial program manager is obvious. Their significance to a government program manager, although perhaps less obvious, is nonetheless every bit as crucial: namely, competition among potential sources is the essence of a program manager's leverage, and the absence of a multiplicity of strong competitors caused by the government's election to provide its own goods and services can only lessen the government program manager's chances of success.

It is thus with guarded optimism that the Final Law of Insatiable Consumption is stated:

> **People working in the private sector should try to save money if at all feasible. There remains a possibility that it may someday be valuable again.**
>
> **(LAW NUMBER XLV)**

Randy Jayne, formerly of the Office of Management and *Budget* and now in private industry, offers the encouraging observation that, "There IS life after government." But unfortunately, much of the evidence is to the contrary. It seems to suggest that eventually the government employs all the people and taxes all their earnings to pay all their wages. In its final stage of development, government becomes the ultimate self-eating watermelon.

I never give anyone hell.
I only tell the truth. They think it's hell.

H. S. TRUMAN

EPILOGUE

If this is the best of possible worlds,
what then are the others?

Voltaire in Candide

Only a field with abundant accomplishments can withstand, perhaps even welcome, intense, critical self-scrutiny and emerge all the stronger. In spite of all the pratfalls and foibles spotlighted in these pages, there are few endeavors in the entire history of mankind that can point to greater achievements than those associated with the aerospace technologies and in particular that subset which has been stimulated by the need to provide for the security of the free world, build a worldwide transportation system, and roll back the frontiers of space.

In 1903, well within the lifetime of many people alive today, Wilbur Wright made that first faltering flight which was eventually to lead not only to today's supersonic aircraft, aircraft which cross the Atlantic in a little over three hours, but also to widebody commercial jets which have changed the entire concept of transportation.

It was less than eight decades from the time the Wright brothers took to the air until the Space Transportation System took to space. . . the latter propelled by fuel carried in a tank so large that the trajectory of Wilbur Wright's famous flight could fit inside it.

Similarly, only five decades elapsed from the time Robert Goddard wrote a paper in 1919 describing how a rocket might be constructed which could reach the moon until Neil Armstrong set foot on the moon, having been placed there by a rocket twice as long as the *altitude* achieved by Goddard's famous rocket less than five decades earlier. The first rocket to propel a man into space some two decades ago was about the same size as the lightning rod attached to the Space Shuttle launch pad. Man has now gone on to explore at close range most of the planets, including conducting detailed analyses of our neighbor, Mars.

In the field of electronics, the Army's Ballistic Research Laboratory was, in 1947, to become the home of the world's first large digital computer, the ENIAC. Weighing 30 tons, employing 18,000 vacuum tubes, filling a large room and consuming the same power that is needed to illuminate some 1,700 light bulbs, the ENIAC less than four decades later has been supplanted by computers which can be bought

237

for a few hundred dollars, carried in one's pocket, and operate sixty times as fast with over ten times the capacity.

Today a single infantryman commands more firepower than entire battalions in earlier eras, being equipped with shoulder-fired antitank missiles and antiaircraft missiles which home in on their intended targets with a precision measured in inches. When called upon in the 1940's to produce large quantities of military equipment, U.S. industry was, within a few tens of months, producing 50,000 aircraft, 80,000 artillery pieces, and 20,000 tanks each year and building liberty ships from start to finish in 90 days.

Much has been accomplished for an industry which traces its beginnings to two people laboring in a bicycle shop and another flying rockets in a cabbage patch—all within the present century.

Yet, each of the laws presented herein results from real-world experience with real-world programs with real-world problems. In spite of past accomplishments, there obviously remains much to be done. Many of the lessons to be learned are self-evident; a few are summarized in the following paragraphs:

- Proposals to start new development programs should receive intense scrutiny, including verification that the need is valid and that the cost of the proposed solution is commensurate with the benefits it offers. Without clear evidence of *significant* payoff, the program should not be started. The objective is to see how many good programs can be completed, not how many programs can be started.

- Once begun, absent truly substantive changes which affect in a very fundamental manner the basis for initiating an effort in the first place, the program should be left alone and maximum stability provided. Turbulence in funding and program guidance adds cost, wastes time, diverts management attention, deters capital investment, increases risk, and demotivates participants. A two-year federal budget would represent a giant step in this regard.

- Debate over the need for a proposed program and the nature of the system involved should be terminated when the point of diminishing returns has been reached. Prolonging the decision process beyond a reasonable point generally leads to only marginally better decisions and often sacrifices perishable technological leadership which has been built-up through great effort in the laboratory. The practice of compressing the "doing time" of a development program to make up for time lost in the indecision process is highly counterproductive.

- Every requirement and every imposed specification should produce real value-added commensurate with its cost. The last few percent of capability, although *sometimes* justified, costs a disproportionate amount.

- Engineering development programs should, in ordinary circumstances, not be initiated until the technology they encompass has been fully demonstrated (with hardware).
- Improving existing systems is often a preferable solution to a need, as compared with beginning an altogether new development. The already incurred costs (sunk costs) and maturity of such existing systems can frequently permit reductions in future costs, schedule and risk in satisfying evolving requirements.
- Extreme capability in terms of performance incorporated into a given item of hardware is frequently an inadequate substitute for larger quantities of somewhat less capable hardware.
- Programs should be *fully* funded, and only those programs which enjoy a high enough priority to demand full funding throughout their existence should be initiated. Spreading limited funding over an excessive number of programs will in the long-term produce less return for the funds invested.
- The program approval and contractor selection processes should be structured to reward *realism*, not *optimism*.
- Competition is the foundation of the enormously successful Free Enterprise system and should be heartily embraced. . . except in those occasional but real cases wherein it may actually increase cost, schedule or risk to an extent that is fundamentally inconsistent with the objectives being sought in the first place.
- All programs should plan for the unexpected and make advance provision, on a probabilistic basis if need be, for adequate resources in terms of time and money to overcome unforeseen problems which do arise.
- The progression of a program from one development or production phase to a succeeding phase should not be keyed to the calendar, but should be triggered by the successful completion of specified precursor milestones. . .usually in the form of tests.
- It is very expensive in time and money to conduct programs "heel-to-toe" with no overlap whatsoever between successive phases. The extent of overlap (concurrency) which is admitted, however, should be based on a careful assessment of exposure in the event unexpected problems do occur late in the predecessor phase. A modest amount of concurrency generally goes a long way.
- The *sine qua non* of successful program execution is the participation of highly competent and highly motivated people. Carefully selected but small groups of individuals can contribute far beyond their numbers and should be rewarded accordingly. . . if for

no reason other than the fact that it is a sound business investment. The imposition of arbitrary pay ceilings on the federal workforce is an example of a counterproductive action.

- Communication is an essential element of program management, especially in large programs. This requires an understanding on the part of the communicator of what message is to be conveyed and a language understandable by all those involved in the communication process. The contract document is, for example, among other things, a critical element of communication and as such should be designed to assure that the objectives it imparts to a contractor, in terms of penalties and rewards, are consistent with those of the sponsor.
- Rules, regulations, and reports are not a substitute for sound judgment. Managers must be given the latitude to manage as well as to be held accountable for their results.
- Excessive layering of one level of management on top of another is expensive, demotivating to the individuals involved and generally counterproductive. Higher-level managers should focus on broader issues having greater potential consequences. Lower levels of management should be permitted the freedom and resources to focus on more detailed matters which are also in the aggregate very consequential to the outcome of an enterprise. As Plato suggested, justice is everyone doing his own job.
- Particular attention must be focused on enhancing the reliability of complex systems. This objective generally cannot be satisfied with awareness campaigns, but rather requires early attention in the design process through the introduction, for example, of redundancy, the elimination of single-point failure modes, derating of components, extensive testing, careful reporting of test results, fixing root-causes of problems encountered, and repeating the test/fix/test/fix process over and over again.
- Thorough environmental test programs should be conducted during the build sequence, progressing from component tests to subsystem tests to complete system tests. The discovery of component problems during system tests is an extremely expensive proposition. Particular vigilance is required not to permit imposed budget reductions to take the form of test reductions.
- Software development requires much the same emphasis and management approach as does hardware development, including careful *a priori* structuring of the task to be performed, close coordination of individual efforts, and thorough testing. Software development most assuredly cannot be set apart as some sort of "off-line" supporting activity treated as an appendage to the hardware effort.

- As in all endeavors, integrity and candor are paramount. Problems not surfaced are likely to remain problems not solved.
- The foremost feature of successful programs is DISCIPLINE. Discipline to forego "nice-to-have" features, discipline to minimize engineering changes, discipline to do thorough failure analyses, discipline to abide by test protocols, and discipline to "tough out" the problems which will occur in even the best-managed, worthwhile programs — and as Robert Townsend put it in his book *Up the Organization*, discipline not to keep pulling up the flowers to see if their roots are healthy. Most of our problems are, as could be their solutions, self-imposed.

So in the Libyan fable it is told
That once an eagle, stricken with a dart,
Said, when he saw the fashion of the shaft,
"With our own feathers, not by others' hands,
Are we now smitten."
Aeschylus

Law is like sausage.
If you like it, you shouldn't watch it being made.

BISMARCK

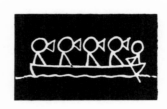

Viking Penguin, Inc. (40 West 23 St., New York, N.Y. 10010) has issued a revised and expanded version of this technical edition for the general market.